Word to the World

Word to the World

Good News to the Nations

Keswick 2011

Edited by Elizabeth McQuoid

Copyright © 2011 Keswick Ministries and Authentic Media Limited

17 16 15 14 13 12 11   7 6 5 4 3 2 1

First published 2011 by Authentic Media Limited
52 Presley Way, Crownhill, Milton Keynes, Bucks., MK8 0ES
www.authenticmedia.co.uk

The right of Elizabeth McQuoid to be identified as the Editor of this Work has been
asserted by her in accordance with the Copyright, Designs and Patents Act 1988

British Library Cataloguing in Publication Data

A catalogue record for this book is available from the
British Library

ISBN 978-1-85078-958-1

Unless otherwise indicated, all Scripture quotations are taken from
The Holy Bible, New International Version (Anglicized edition)
Copyright © 1979, 1984 by Biblica (formerly International Bible society).
Used by permission of Hodder & Stoughton Publishers an Hachette UK
company. All rights reserved.
Scripture quotations marked (ESV) are from The Holy Bible, English
Standard Version, published by HarperCollins Publishers © 2001 Crossway
Bibles, a publishing ministry of Good News Publishers. Used by
permission. All rights reserved.
Scripture quotations marked (NKJV) are from the Holy Bible, New King
James Version. Copyright © 1982 by Thomas Nelson, Inc. Used by
permission. All rights reserved.
Scripture taken from *The Message*. Copyright © 1993, 1994, 1995, 1996, 2000,
2001, 2002. Used by permission of NavPress Publishing Group.

Cover design by David Smart
Photographs by Neil Edbrooke and Sam Townshend
Printed and bound by CPI Group (UK) Ltd., Croydon, CR0 4YY

Contents

The Seminars

The Word @ 2.30

The Addresses

Introduction by the Chairman of the 2011 Convention

The theme of this book could not be more urgent for Christians today. All around the world the Word of God is advancing, sustaining the trajectory described in Luke's account in the book of Acts - 'the word of God continued to spread and increase' (see Acts 6:7). In the global south the Word of God is specially needed to strengthen and nurture the growing multitudes who are coming to faith. In the West, the Word is specially needed to penetrate the nominalism of the churches and to challenge the prevailing secular and materialist world views. And for all believers, the Word needs to come freshly, day by day, transforming our lives as it brings us into God's presence.

Keswick 2011 proved to be an extraordinary eye-opener, as the dynamic combination of Bible exposition, global prayer, practical seminars, Earthworks exhibitions, challenging preaching and the call to missions impacted some 12,000 people. Our hope is that, in this selection of addresses, you will feel something of that same dynamic impact. I would specially like to thank the various speakers for their willingness to allow their material to go into print, and to thank Elizabeth McQuoid for her editing of the material.

May the Word of the Lord speed on and triumph in our lives, our churches and our world.

Jonathan Lamb
Chairman

The Bible Readings

God's missionary heart

by Ajith Fernando

Ajith Fernando

Ajith Fernando has been National Director of Youth for Christ in Sri Lanka since 1976. These days his main responsibilities are mentoring leaders, and teaching staff and volunteers. He ministers to Christian workers and others through a counselling and Bible teaching ministry in Sri Lanka and abroad. Ajith has written 14 books which have been translated into 18 different languages. *The Call to Joy and Pain* was awarded the *Christianity Today* Book of the Year Award for church and pastoral leadership.

God's missionary heart: Jonah 4:1–11

Psalm 85:6 says, 'Will you not revive us again, that your people may rejoice in you?' (ESV) and if God uses a preacher as the instrument of revival usually the preacher is the one who's most elated. But chapter 4 of Jonah begins, 'But it displeased Jonah exceedingly, and he was angry' (ESV). God had brought about an amazing revival and the preacher, Jonah, was unhappy about it, even angry.

And so he prayed to the Lord and asked God to take away his life. In the Bible you often find God's people complaining to him. The complaint is never glorified or justified though, often it is met with a very gentle rebuke from God. It is foolish to doubt God's ways, his wisdom and his sovereignty, but we are weak people and we do. The best thing is to face up to the reality of confusion and go to God with the problem.

This Jonah did, and we can thank God for that. Moses did that when he complained about the burdens of leadership. Jeremiah did that when he complained about his loneliness. Asaph did that when he was talking in Psalm 73 about the wicked prospering. And God always ministers to people like that. In the Scriptures you get deep theological truth that comes as a result of the questionings of God's people. So we fault Jonah for his attitudes but we can at least commend him for his honesty in expressing his doubts.

Some orthodox people who have the right belief are afraid to be honest with their doubts. They won't grapple with their doubts, they just suppress them. Often they become intellectually defensive and people sense a lack of authentic faith. God is not intimidated by our doubts so don't be afraid to go to him with them. You will emerge with a deeper understanding of God's ways and he will minister to you.

Let's look at Jonah's prayer. 'O LORD, is not this what I said when I was yet in my country? That is why I made haste to flee to Tarshish; for I knew that you are a gracious God and merciful, slow to anger and abounding in steadfast love, and relenting from disaster' (4:2, ESV). He's revolting against the doctrine of God's mercy.

Jonah is repeating a very common Jewish creed which appeared first in Exodus 34:6. We know Jonah knew his creeds well from his prayer in chapter 2. The creed he uses here is quoted often in the Old Testament and the key phrase is 'abounding in steadfast love'. 'Steadfast love' is *hesed* in Hebrew, a term usually used to speak about God's covenant love for Israel. Israel's people enjoyed a special relationship with God which was described in terms of a covenant or a testament. And included in that was God's loyalty to Israel – his faithfulness to his covenant. But many Jews regarded *hesed* as a privilege reserved for the Jews; they didn't want to extend it to the Gentiles. And this, of course, is not what was originally intended in the call of Israel. The Jews were called to be a light to the Gentiles. But Jonah didn't want to extend God's love to the Gentiles.

I live in a country that has been torn by ethnic strife, and one of the sad realizations I have made is that prejudice is one of the last things touched in the process of sanctification. Very often, people who are evangelicals, who believe the Bible and say they are not racist, would consider people of another race as inferior, wrong or bad. Nineveh is in modern Iraq and there's a lot of anger towards Muslims today. But the great commission extends to them also. The primary way Christians should look at Muslims is as people who need the Saviour. In 2 Corinthians 5:14,16 Paul says, 'For the love of Christ controls us, because we have concluded this: that one has died for all, therefore all have died . . . From now on, therefore, we regard no one according to the flesh. Even though we once regarded Christ according to the flesh' (ESV). He is saying now we don't look at people as

Muslim, English, white, or black. The primary way we are to look at people is given in 2 Corinthians 5:17, 'Therefore, if anyone is in Christ, he is a new creation. The old has passed away; behold, the new has come' (ESV). So we look at someone and if they are a believer, 'Oh, you are my brother or sister in Christ', and if they are an unbeliever, 'How can I tell this person about Jesus?'

Now salvation has come to Nineveh but Jonah is mad at God. You know, this is a very common thing even among Christians. If you are bitter with someone you get angry with those who help that person. And if it is God who helps that person you get angry with God. Even Christians want their enemies punished and if someone is kind to them they take it as a personal insult. I have seen people leave churches because of this. They call it justice: 'You know we are leaving because of justice.' But what if God related to us like that? Jonah had rebelled knowing God's will and now he's angry that God forgave people who repented; they hardly knew God's will but when they were told it, they repented and now he's rebelling - he's angry about their conversion. In chapter 3:10 we are told that God turned away from his anger and in 4:1 we are told Jonah was angry. You see, when you harbour anger over enemies, you may be on the exact opposite side to God and that's a very dangerous place to be. Even leaders like Jonah can act wrongly when things don't go their way. They want something to happen; it doesn't happen and they can be so wrong in their reaction to that.

So Jonah starts his creed saying, 'You are a gracious God and merciful, slow to anger and abounding in steadfast love' (v.2, ESV). It is because God is gracious and merciful that he shows covenant love to Israel. They don't deserve it, they didn't merit salvation; it was all an act of mercy. And it's the same with Christianity. The gospel, our salvation, is because of grace not because of works (Eph. 2:8–9). So we cannot boast about our salvation; it is God's free gift, and faith is just accepting this gift. Jonah seems to have thought that the Jews deserved salvation and Nineveh did not. And those who think they earn salvation believe they have grounds for boasting. They think they deserve God's favour more than wicked people and therefore they are not happy when mercy is extended to these unworthy people.

This was, of course, the attitude of the elder brother who told his father, 'Look, these many years I have served you' (Luke 15:29, ESV). The Greek says, 'slaving'. He was a slave, not a son! His boast was his work, not God's grace. Those who are aware of grace are joyful people. It is very interesting that in the Greek there is a sequence of words all beginning with the consonants *ch* and *r*. There is *charis* which is grace, and of course, *charisma* which is gift. And because of *charis* and *charisma* we have *eucharistia* which is thanksgiving. And then because of this thanksgiving there is *chara* which is joy. You know, God has shown *charis* to us, grace to us, and we are thankful, and people who are thankful are joyful people. And then there is *charizomai* which is that you freely give, or you forgive. Because of grace, we are joyful and the joy makes us freely give to people, to forgive people and to enjoy grace in others.

Now Jonah was wrong thinking he deserved salvation and he was also wrong thinking the Ninevites didn't. There are some people we dislike, and though we never say it, we think, 'Don't go preaching the gospel to those people, they are not worthy of salvation.' About ten years ago I ushered in the New Year at our drug rehab centre with the students. After we had finished the service we were in the dorm chatting. One of the students there talked about his previous life. He said he would sleep most of the day, get up at night and rob a house. He would sell what he had stolen and with that money get more drugs and go to sleep. This was his daily routine and, as he was saying this, I thought to myself, this is the type of person that I would be so mad at if they came to my house as a robber and now he's my brother. Recently we had a Sponsors' Day to thank our sponsors and he gave his testimony. Now he's married, he has a child, he's doing his own little vegetable business, going on with the Lord, and active in his church. Here was a person we would have thought totally unworthy of salvation but as Romans 5:8 says, 'But God shows his love for us in that while we were still sinners, Christ died for us' (ESV). God didn't wait for us to be worthy because he knew that we did not have the ability to be worthy.

Now we come, in verse 3, to a bigger surprise, Jonah says, 'Now, O LORD, please take my life from me, for it is better for me to die than to live' (ESV). Incidentally, there are other people of God who have wanted to die: Elijah, when he was exhausted after the big battle and found out Queen Jezebel was trying to kill him, said he wanted to die. Jeremiah, when he was lonely and rejected, cursed the day he was born. So if there is anyone here who has thought to themselves, 'it is better for me to die', you are in very good company. Some of God's great servants have felt the same way.

Jonah's reason, of course, was he had a theological problem. He was in despair because his theology was correct but his personal desire clashed with what he knew to be God's will. His theology and his heart were at loggerheads. His heart says, 'I and my people are better than other people, we deserve to be saved.' His head said, 'Salvation is an unmerited gift, given because of God's mercy. The Ninevites need to hear it, just like the Israelites need to hear it.' There was a conflict within him. He had lost the *shalom* – the peace of God that comes from God's rule and gives wholeness to our lives.

And this is the misery of disobedient orthodox people; sometimes it's worse than the misery of those who have rejected the gospel altogether. The orthodox know what God's power is, they know they can't fight God, but their hearts do not want to follow God's ways. Let me give you two examples. One is when somebody loves a non-believer and wants to get married to them. Their heart says, 'I want to marry this person', but their head says, 'No, this is wrong.' And there's this clash inside them.

The other example is if someone has hurt you. Your heart tells you to nurture these wounds and meditate on them. And so you're planning this pity party: you sit in your room, planning to have a wonderful time thinking about how bad people are to you. And then God comes and ruins the whole party by saying that it's going to be turned into something good in your life and you need to forgive. So the head says, 'God will turn this to good so forgive', but the heart says, 'No, I must nurture this, this is my friend, this is what gives me identity, people have been bad to me.'

My dear friends, it's much better to get our identity from the fact that God has been good to us than that people have been bad to us. What a desperate situation to be in: to know the truth but not want to follow it; to know the folly of disagreeing with God but not be able to agree with him. The conflict becomes unbearable; you just want to give up and die.

Now it's very interesting, in verse 3 Jonah says, 'it's better for me to die' (ESV). The Hebrew translation is, 'it's good for me to die.' And in verse 4, also, where it says, 'Do you do well to be angry?' (ESV). Again, it's the word 'good'. So Jonah says, 'it is good for me to die', and God replies, 'Is it good for you to be angry?' Jonah questions God for not being angry at the Ninevites and God questions Jonah for being angry. It shows how opposite our thinking can be when we are away from God.

When we come to verses 5 to 8 there's an experience with a plant. Verse 5 says, 'Jonah went out of the city and sat to the east of the city and made a booth for himself there' (ESV). He sat under the shelter but it was obviously inadequate because he was really happy when the plant came and gave him some shade. Why is he watching what is happening to the city? We don't know. Was he hoping that God would change his mind and destroy Nineveh? Was he waiting for some action from God to explain his ways more clearly? We are not told. But we are told in verse 6 that God appoints a plant: 'Now the LORD God appointed the plant and made it come over Jonah, that it might be a shade over his head, to save him from his discomfort' (ESV). We don't know what kind of plant it was; some people think it's a castor oil plant, but we can't be sure.

Now Jonah's response is most interesting. The second half of verse 6 says, 'So Jonah was exceedingly glad because of the plant' (ESV). He was terribly pleased. Jonah was terribly upset when the Gentiles are saved and now he's terribly pleased when he's looked after. This is the attitude of people whose satisfaction comes from things, not from God. Jonah regarded the vine as an acknowledgement of his inherent worth: 'I deserve God's help and here is evidence of that. This is the way God should be treating me.' But if you trust in yourself and your affirmation comes from people and things you are trusting in something very insecure. Have you seen people like this? One day they are right up, praising God and so happy. The next day some small thing happens and they're angry with the church and calling everybody hypocrites. This happens when your joy is not in God. When these people are affirmed they are full of joy. When they see others, rather than themselves, affirmed they get very upset.

When your trust is in God there is a quiet confidence. You know that what's important is not how I do, what people think of me, what I get, or what I don't get. What's important is, 'I belong to God' and 'God is my God, he loves me not because of anything inherent in me, he loves me because he loves me.' That is the basis of God's love and we can trust him to look after us. To such believers, the greatest source of joy is not things that happen to them but just the fact that God loves them.

Verse 7: 'But when the dawn came up the next day, God appointed a worm that attacked the plant, so that it withered' (ESV). God is appointing here - he appointed a fish in 1:17, a plant in 4:6 – and now he has appointed a worm to discipline Jonah. God is teaching Jonah in a most graphic way. He had been complaining that God didn't destroy Nineveh. That didn't mean that God was incapable of destruction; he could destroy, and he appoints a worm to destroy Jonah's shelter.

Actually, a few years later, Assyria is going to be appointed to destroy Israel. So this is a real-life parable for Jonah – God is both loving and holy. He can provide a plant to give shade but he can also, through his holiness, bless people in other ways. God not only blesses people with what they regard as good and makes them comfortable; sometimes he blesses people by chastising them, by disciplining them, through discomfort, pain and heartache. And the discipline serves to teach a lesson, to burn off impurity in our lives. Chastisement and discipline from God are a clear example of God's holy love, and, of course, the clearest example of holy love is the cross of Christ. In Proverbs 3:12 we are told that the Lord reproves or disciplines those in whom he delights (also in Hebrews 12:6).

Those of you from the Salvation Army may know the name Albert Orsborn. Albert Orsborn was, at one time, the general of the Salvation Army and their best known poet. As a young officer in London God really blessed his work, many people came to know Christ through his ministry and the division grew a lot. After some time, another officer told him he'd heard they were going to divide his division and said, 'Don't allow it because that will reduce your impact and influence.' Orsborn said he would accept what his superiors wanted but he developed an attitude of arguing.

He said, 'I was fighting, not for the Kingdom, but for my position in the Kingdom, and God was not pleased. The Spirit was grieved by my behaviour, and when the Spirit grieves, the Spirit leaves.' And although he went through the motions of ministry he was an angry person. Others may have thought he was doing his work just as before but he knew that the anointing had left him; there wasn't the freshness of God's Spirit working through him.

Then he had an accident and had to stay in hospital for several days. While he was in hospital, God began to speak to him and show him the selfishness that had ruined his spirit. One day, in the next room he heard people singing some songs. They were singing of the joys he once knew – he wept, repented, came back to God and God was able to use him again.

He wrote a beautiful poem about his experience saying to God if the gold gets mixed with dross, if self comes into my service, don't stop me from serving. And what's the solution he recommends to God? Lord, if dross comes into my life send me through a stern cleansing so that through it I may be able to bring joy to you again.

Well, that's what happens to poor Jonah in verse 8 – when the sun rose, God appointed a scorching east wind which beat down on Jonah's head so he was faint and asked that he might die. He said, 'It is better for me to die than to live' (ESV). We don't know what this wind was – some people think it was a sirocco wind – we aren't sure. But the wind plus the sun is unbearable and Jonah wants to die. Earlier he wanted to die because God had treated the Gentiles in a nice way; now he wants to die because God has treated him in the same way he wants God to treat the Gentiles. You can imagine his frustration. He has a stubborn heart and God is trying to reach out to it. He has to be brought to the end of himself before the great message of this book can be taught. In verse 9 God questions Jonah again, 'Do you do well to be angry for the plant?' (ESV) And he said, 'Yes, I do well to be angry, angry enough to die' (ESV). Jonah is snapping back at God and

God's answer is so typical. Instead of rebuking he gently but firmly reasons with Jonah.

We often see this gentle firmness in the way God responds to people. God disciplines us but he does so wisely. He knows how much we can handle and what is best for us. He never lowers his standards but he varies his tone without varying his demands. And that is what he does here. The Lord said, 'You pity the plant, for which you did not labour, nor did you make it grow, which came into being in a night and perished in a night' (ESV). What he's saying is: you had no deep tie with this plant that withered; you did nothing for it; you had no investment in it; it came up suddenly and died suddenly, yet you seem to be concerned about the plant.

God explains his relationship with Nineveh is much more serious than Jonah's relationship with the plant. He says, in verse 11, 'Should I not pity Nineveh, that great city, in which there are more than 120,000 persons who do not know their right hand from their left, and also much cattle?' (ESV) God is concerned for the Ninevites who don't know how to make moral judgements. Jesus responded similarly when he saw that the crowds were 'harassed and helpless, like sheep without a shepherd' (Matt. 9:36, ESV). We are told that Jesus was moved to the depths of his being. In Nineveh there were 120,000 people all made in the image of God and so God's concern and compassion is expressed here: 'Should I not pity them? Should I not be concerned?'

This is what Paul says about the Jews in Romans 9:2–3, 'I have great sorrow and unceasing anguish in my heart. For I could wish that I myself were accursed, and cut off from Christ for the sake of my brothers, my kinsmen according to the flesh' (ESV). What a contrast Jonah is! The Jews had rejected Paul and the gospel but he was willing to die to take the gospel to them. Jonah also wanted to die, but he wanted to die because God had accepted these people into his family.

Jonah was asked to leave his comfort zone and take God's message – he did so unhappily. The attitude of Jonah is seen a lot today; deep down many are not willing to pay the price to get different kinds of people into the family of God. They don't want to change; some people don't even want their churches to grow, because they are comfortable the way they are, the way they do church.

I love the story of an American church situated next to a university. There were no university students coming to the church so the congregation began to pray that somehow God would open the door and some of these university students would want to come in.

It was the hippy era when people used to go without shoes and dress in unkempt ways. And one day one of these guys walked in with no shoes. And he walked right up to the front, came up to the platform where the pastor was preaching, sat down near the pastor and listened.

There was an old elder in the church who saw this and he began to follow this young man. The members of the church thought, 'I wonder what he's going to do now. This guy's without shoes and he's sitting on the platform.' The old man came and sat down beside the young man and listened to the sermon with him.

Anything, anything so that these people can come to Jesus. Anything – any hardship, any difficulty, any challenge to our budget, whatever it is, so that they will come to know God. How did Jonah respond? We are not told. Perhaps the writer deliberately leaves us hanging because some will accept and some will reject.

There's a lovely book on Jonah called *You! Jonah!* written by Thomas John Carlisle. He ends the book with Jonah stalking off into the shade and waiting for God to come around to his way of thinking. Carlisle says that it's actually God who is waiting – waiting for a host of Jonahs to come around to his way of loving. May we come around to God's way of loving.

Proclaiming God's Saviour

by Chris Wright

Chris Wright

Chris Wright was born in Belfast, Northern Ireland. He taught in India 1983–88, and then at All Nations Christian College, where he was Principal from 1993–2001. He is now the International Director of Langham Partnership International, which provides literature, scholarships and preaching training for Majority World pastors and seminaries. His books include *Old Testament Ethics for the People of God*, *The Mission of God*, and *The Mission of God's People*.

Proclaiming God's saviour: Deuteronomy 4 and Acts 4

We have been thinking over the last few mornings about how the mission of God and our mission for God involve how we live and what we do. But our mission also has to do with what we say. We are to know certain things about God, about the Lord Jesus Christ, and we are to proclaim what we know about him. And so our theme this morning is 'Proclaiming God's Saviour' and I want to bring together two texts: Acts 4 and Deuteronomy 4. I am going to read a few verses from each of these chapters and would like you to be thinking about what they have in common.

Here is Deuteronomy 4:32–35,39. This is Moses challenging the people of God to think about their history and past:

> Ask now about the former days, long before your time, from the day God created man on the earth; ask from one end of the heavens to the other. Has anything so great as this ever happened, or has anything like it ever been heard of? Has any other people heard the voice of God speaking out of fire, as you have, and lived? Has any god ever tried to take for himself one nation out of another nation, by testings, by miraculous signs and wonders, by war, by a mighty hand and an outstretched arm, or by great and awesome deeds, like all the things the LORD your God did for you in Egypt before your very eyes? You were

shown these things so that you might know that the LORD is God;
besides him there is no other . . . Acknowledge and take to heart this
day that the LORD is God in heaven above and on the earth below.
There is no other.

Turn now to Acts 4. In chapter 3 Peter has healed a crippled man at
the temple, gets into trouble and is hauled before the Sanhedrin. I am
picking up the story in Acts 4:5:

The next day the rulers, elders and teachers of the law met in
Jerusalem. Annas the high priest was there, and so were Caiaphas, John,
Alexander and the other men of the high priest's family. They had Peter
and John brought before them and began to question them: 'By what
power or what name did you do this?' Then Peter, filled with the Holy
Spirit, said to them: 'Rulers and elders of the people! If we are being
called to account today for an act of kindness shown to a cripple and
are asked how he was healed, then know this, you and all the people
of Israel: It is by the name of Jesus Christ of Nazareth, whom you crucified but whom God raised from the dead, that this man stands before
you healed. He is 'the stone you builders rejected, which has become
the capstone.' Salvation is found in no one else, for there is no other
name under heaven given to men by which we must be saved.

What do these passages have in common? Both of them are situations
of conflict and challenge. In Acts the conflict is between on the one
hand those who were claiming, as Peter and John were, that Jesus of
Nazareth was the Messiah who had been crucified but was risen and
exalted, and on the other hand those who rejected any such dangerous nonsense about Jesus and would not listen. And in Deuteronomy
there was going to be conflict between the faith of Israel in Yahweh
their unique covenant God who they were called to worship alone,
and the polytheistic religion of all the other gods and idols of Canaan
in the land into which they were going.

And what we have in both Acts and Deuteronomy is that the
speakers refer to unique events that have been witnessed and that lead
to certain conclusions about God and the Lord Jesus Christ. In both

cases the claims that are made about God, the God of Israel in the Old Testament, and about Jesus in the New Testament, are presented as non-negotiable, universal, and based on something that has actually happened. So it is a situation of conflict in the Old Testament and in the New Testament. And I don't need to tell you that we live in a situation of conflict today in which Christians are called upon to express who we are, what we believe and why our faith matters in the midst of all sorts of rival claims and conflicting loyalties – whether those are of other religious faiths, resurgent atheism, or just sheer apathy. As in the days of the apostles so today there are those who reject Jesus and any claim that he is the Lord. There are many in our world who haven't even heard the name of Jesus let alone had the opportunity to reject or accept him. So knowing the living God is a privilege God has entrusted to us, and then the responsibility of making him known in the midst of competing claims in the world, that is also part of our mission. We are commanded to know the truth about God, to live the truth about God, and also to speak – to declare the truth about the living God and the Lord Jesus Christ.

So with that by way of introduction, let's think first about the undeniable experiences that both passages speak of. In Acts we see a man healed and a man raised – both of them undeniable. Acts chapter 3 tells a story about a man, crippled all his life, who was healed and how that then led to an immediate, opportunistic piece of evangelism in which Peter and John speak to the crowd. They explain that Jesus of Nazareth, whom they had seen crucified a few weeks earlier, was in fact the Messiah, the God of Israel, the God of their ancestors. He was the one who had been promised to them. The healing of this cripple was a sign of the exaltation of Jesus and they must come to repent and to have faith in him (Acts 3:25–26).

And then in Acts chapter 4 the shock waves of that message run through the Jewish establishment. The leaders, the Sanhedrin, thought they had dealt with Jesus. They had taken him to the place of execution, they had opened the door of death and pushed him through, and slammed it shut. Finished, they had thought. But now they are hearing that this Jesus who was crucified, God has raised him from the dead. So they called Peter and John to account for this preaching. But what Luke points out so well and almost humorously, is that while they were there trying to deny the resurrection of Jesus they could not deny the guy standing in the corner – the man who had been healed. For all his life they had passed him at the gate, crippled, on the floor, unable to walk, and now he is standing in the room. And we read in verses 14–16 that 'since they could see the man who had been healed standing there with them, there was nothing they could say. So they ordered them to withdraw from the Sanhedrin and then conferred together. "What are we going to do with these men?" they asked. "Everybody living in Jerusalem knows they have done an outstanding miracle, and we cannot deny it."' It was undeniable. They could not deny the reality of what everyone had seen and witnessed.

Now the significant thing is that Peter has been preaching the resurrection of Jesus on exactly the same basis. If you look back at chapter 3:15 Peter says, 'You killed the author of life, but God raised him from the dead. We are witnesses of this.' We have seen this. We cannot deny it, you cannot deny it – we have seen it. And all through Peter is presenting the resurrection of Jesus as a public, witnessed, historical event. It's as if he is saying to the Sanhedrin, 'Look, you guys are witnesses of a healing; we are witnesses of a resurrection. You have seen a man healed and you cannot deny it. We've seen a man raised and we cannot deny it.' So it is an undeniable experience on the basis of which the gospel is being preached.

We need to remind ourselves that the whole Christian faith is based on this publicly witnessed historical event of the resurrection of the Lord Jesus Christ. The Christian faith is not our speculation or our spirituality or 'how I have found God and you could too if you had the same kind of faith as me'. The gospel is good news. It is not a good idea. It is not good advice. It is good news about something that has happened which has been undeniably witnessed. Part of our problem and one of the reasons why we find Christian witness often difficult is that we have allowed ourselves to privatize our faith. Just as our culture for the past 200 years has been separating public and private realms, sacred and secular realms, so we have accepted the resurrection of Jesus and taken it out of public truth and confined it to private piety. And really we aren't aware of how much we have done it.

Many of us probably grew up singing a very happy chorus which asks how we know Jesus lives. And the answer given is – he lives within my heart. Now that is true – praise God we believe in the indwelling power of the living Christ in our hearts. But that was not the message that the apostles went into Jerusalem to preach. If they had gone around saying, 'Jesus whom you had crucified is living in our hearts,' the Jewish authorities would have said, 'As long as he's still in the grave you can have him in your heart as long as you like.' You see, the message of the resurrection of Jesus is not personal piety about us and our experience of Jesus inside. It is the message of the truth of the gospel as an undeniable, witnessed event in history. The living God raised Jesus from the dead. We need to get back to that confidence in the '*having happenedness*' of the gospel.

When we read what Moses has to say in Deuteronomy 4 he does the same thing. He addresses the people of Israel just before they move into the land of promise and he wants to remind them of the unique events in their history they had just lived through, that they had just witnessed (v.35). He even challenges them to do a vast research project. He says, you can look from the beginning of human history, from the day God created people on the earth, you can look through the whole of space and time, from one end of the heavens to the other – and you will not find anything like this God who has revealed himself at Mount Sinai and has brought you out of Egypt (Deut. 4:33–34).

What Moses is claiming is that what God has done in the Exodus and at Mount Sinai was completely unprecedented. God had never done anything like that before. God had not done it for any other nation. So Moses is saying that Israel's experience of the living God is unique. God had revealed himself to Israel in a way that he had not revealed himself to any other people and he had redeemed Israel in a way that no other people knew as yet. Now, of course, that is not to deny, because the Old Testament does not deny, that the living God can speak to any human being, that there is a knowledge of God throughout the earth, that people have some understanding of God's moral demands and even that God has moved on the face of the planet in many other places as well. But what Moses is saying is, 'Israelites, you have an experience of the living God – of his revelation at Mount Sinai and of his salvation in the Exodus.' The Exodus was this unique gospel-saving event by which God had brought his people out of Egypt and in the Sinai he had made known his name, his character, his covenant, his worship – there is an overflow of the revelation of God there. And Moses says, 'You know these things, you have seen these things - this is a reality.'

So both Peter and John in Acts, and Moses in Deuteronomy, appeal to facts. They appeal to witnessed experience as the basis to their claim about God and about Jesus. And when we go out in mission, part of what we are doing is sharing something we know about God. Not because it is our opinion or we have had a mystical experience but we are sharing what God has done, things that have happened, how God has acted to bring about the salvation of the world. And that is another reason why we need to have confidence in the Bible. Moses was able to say to the Israelites, 'You have seen these things, you have experienced these things.' Peter and John said, 'We cannot deny what we have seen and heard.' Well, of course, we weren't there and are therefore dependent upon those who have given us the record of these events in Scripture. The Old Testament records the saving acts of God in Israel, and the New Testament the gospels and stories of the Lord Jesus Christ. We are dependent upon the testimony of Scripture for the undeniable experiences they describe.

Well, that leads us on, secondly, to the uncompromising claims that are made in both texts. And I wondered if you spotted that phrase, 'no other'? 'No other name', say Peter and John in Acts 4. 'No other God', says Moses in Deuteronomy.

Let's start first in Deuteronomy 4. 'No other' – that is what Moses says twice. In verse 35: 'You were shown these things so that you might know that the LORD is God; besides him there is no other' and again in verse 39, 'Acknowledge and take to heart . . . that the LORD is God in heaven above and on the earth below. There is no other.'

All that Israel had experienced of these historical events was so that they would learn something utterly vital to their faith, and that is the identity of the Lord Yahweh – the one and only living God. And Moses is saying he is the only God there is and you know this now because of what God has done for you. That is their privilege. That is also their responsibility.

So Old Testament Israel knew God in a way no other nation did, and sometimes this is described as monotheism: the belief that there is only one God. But the point of this text is not just arithmetic. Believing only one God exists is a good thing but it is not what this text actually says. It is not the arithmetic of how many Gods there are – it is the identity. Merely believing in one God is not enough, but knowing who the living God is, is what counts. The Lord is God. And Yahweh the Lord God is the God who has already shown himself in this story. He is a God of compassion and justice, the God of salvation, the God of revelation, the God who has brought Israel out of slavery. The God who says to the Israelites, 'You must now know me and love me and serve me exclusively.' So the text then does not just show who God really is but what God is really like. It is this God – Yahweh God – who is God and there is no other.

If Deuteronomy says that there is no other God, Peter and John say in Acts 4 there is no other Saviour – 'Salvation is found in no one else, for there is no other name under heaven given to men by which we must be saved' (Acts 4:12). Now what makes this astonishing is that Peter was talking about Jesus when he said those words. Rather than naming God, Jews just said 'the name' and if Peter had been speaking about Yahweh, the God of Israel, then the words he says here could as easily have been written in the Old Testament as in the New. In fact, Isaiah more or less says exactly this. In Isaiah 45 God says, 'There is no God apart from me, a righteous God and a Saviour; there is none but me. Turn to me and be saved, all you ends of the earth; for I am God, and there is no other' (vv. 21–22). And here Peter says there is no other name given under heaven by which we must be saved than the name of Yahweh, the Lord God of Israel. If Peter had said that, nobody in the room would have disagreed with him. The Sanhedrin would have said, 'Absolutely. We all believe that.' But of course the shock, the offence, is that he wasn't talking about Yahweh, the God of Israel – or was he? You see, the point is that Peter was a Jew. Peter knew these words, he knew what he was saying. And for any Jew to speak about 'the name' and 'no other' and 'salvation' was to speak God language.

This is Isaiah language. And so, the offence is that he is taking this language which he and all his hearers would have known could only apply to the living God and applying it to Jesus. Jesus is now the name that carries the same unique saving power as the sovereign Lord God of Israel who is Saviour of the nations according to Isaiah. That is a very early confession of Peter right at the beginning of Acts but it develops through the rest of the New Testament.

In Philippians 2:9–11 Paul also uses the language of 'the name'. Paul, possibly quoting an early Christian hymn, speaks about how Jesus came down from heaven, made himself nothing, became human, became a servant, went to the cross and therefore God has highly exalted him and given him the name that is above every name. For any Jew there was only one name that was above every other name and that was Yahweh, Adonai, Kurios, the Lord. And the hymn goes on, 'God has exalted him to the highest place and given him the name that is above every other name, that at the name belonging to Jesus' – which I think is how it should be translated – not just 'at the name Jesus', but 'at the name Jesus now has, every knee should bow on heaven and on earth and every tongue confess that Jesus is Kurios, Lord, to the glory of God the Father.' The early Christian hymn writer was quoting Isaiah 45:23–24. God says about himself, 'By myself I have sworn . . . Before me every knee will bow; by me every tongue will swear. They will say of me, "In the LORD alone are righteousness and strength."'

And so in Peter's speech, in Paul's writing and in early Christian hymns, they were taking the language, originally written about the Lord God of Israel, the one and only living God and Saviour, and applying it to Jesus: 'This is Jesus of Nazareth whom you crucified, but whom God has raised from the dead and we are proclaiming him to you.' That is the authority of their mission and the message of their mission.

So we have been thinking about the undeniable experiences that are in both texts and about the uncompromising claim that is made in the text for God and the Lord Jesus Christ. And that brings us finally to the undivided loyalty that both texts require. From Deuteronomy 4 we see that Israel had some unique experiences of God on the basis of which they know who God is and are entrusted with the knowledge of the uniqueness and universality of the living God. And what we see in the New Testament text is that by using exactly the same language in the same way the New Testament affirms that Jesus of Nazareth is the one who embodies both the uniqueness of Israel – this Old Testament people of God – because he is the Messiah of Israel, and so he embodies their identity and mission, and he embodies the Lord God of Israel in his incarnation. So what we are now called to do is to know these things, to believe these things and then to make them known. And that calls for loyalty. It means we need to recognize these things are true and then we have no option but to make them known. Our mission is a reflex of what we now know to be true about God.

And so that is why I say that this uncompromising claim, this loyalty we have to have to these truths, it is something we have to take to the world. But I hope you can see what we are claiming is nothing to do with ourselves. It is not about how wonderful Christians are, how great a religion we have, and the answers we have come up with for the world's problems. No, it is not a claim about ourselves, it is simply a witness and a testimony to what the Scriptures – the Old and the New Testament – tell us about the one true living God and how, and where, and through whom this living God has acted in order to bring salvation to us and to the whole of creation. That testimony is then based upon the historical events and the witness of the Scriptures. So if we know these things then we must go and share them.

And that is, of course, what we find in both the Acts and the Deuteronomy passage. In Acts, the apostles are confronted with people who knew that if what the apostles were saying was true, then it changed everything. It changed their whole world, their power and their status. But Peter and John weren't going to be silenced by that. They could not deny the truth of what they had seen and heard (vv.19–20).

They were saying if Christ has been crucified for us, if raised from the dead, if God was in Christ reconciling the world to himself, then we cannot keep silent about these things. They have to be told. And we have that same requirement in our mission. Either Jesus is the only Saviour and Lord of the world or he is not. But if he is, then with Peter and John we are called to stand up for him with loyalty and unwavering witness, no matter what the hostility, the enmity, the persecution or just the sheer apathy of the world around us.

If you go back to Deuteronomy, you find the same emphasis about loyal love for the Lord. We have looked at the verses in Deuteronomy 4 about what Israel was to know. And then in 6:4–5 we read, 'Hear, O Israel: The LORD our God, the LORD is one. Love the LORD your God with all your heart and with all your soul and with all your strength.' That love is to be a total commitment of mind, will, emotions, and energy to the Lord. So one Lord, one love, one loyalty – that is the message of Deuteronomy. One Lord, one name, one Saviour – that is the challenge of the story in Acts.

And that is the biblical gospel. It tells us there are unique and undeniable things that God has done in the Scriptures culminating in the life, death and resurrection of the Lord Jesus Christ of Nazareth. And it then goes on to make these uncompromising claims and says that in these events the living God has acted to save humanity, to redeem his whole creation, and there is no other God, and no other source of salvation. And that therefore makes claims on us – the undivided loyalty of our hearts, our minds, our lives and our wills, to go out and make those things known to the world around us. As we see from both Deuteronomy and Acts that is the mission God calls us to – in our world and in our generation, for his name and glory.

The promise of life in the face of death

by Peter Maiden

Peter Maiden

Peter Maiden is a Trustee of Keswick Ministries and International Director of Operation Mobilization. He travels extensively to fulfil his commitment with OM, which has staff serving in 116 countries. Peter serves on the board of a number of other Christian groups, is a member of Hebron Evangelical Church in Carlisle and an Honorary Canon of Carlisle Cathedral. Peter enjoys family life with his wife, Win, and their three grown-up children and eight grandchildren.

The promise of life in the face of death: 2 Timothy 1

Our dear brother John Stott went to be with the Lord last week and we were told that in his final hours he did two things along with his colleagues and close family members. They listened to certain parts of Handel's *Messiah* and then John asked that 2 Timothy be read to him. The last actions, the last words of a person are often considered to be of great significance.

I want us to look in these five mornings at the last words of someone else: the last words of the apostle Paul. And as we do so we are looking at the last words of a missionary, probably the greatest missionary the world has ever witnessed. This man's passion to see the Word taken to the whole world is evident. It is evident throughout his life and throughout his teaching. We are looking over the last words of a totally, utterly committed missionary.

Let's begin by looking briefly at the background to the letter. How does Paul's situation here fit in with what we know of the rest of his life? How do you fit it into Luke's account of Paul's travels in the Acts of the Apostles? It is rather difficult to fit 2 Timothy into Dr Luke's account in Acts. It is by no means everyone's view, but I believe that there is strong evidence for concluding Paul was released from the imprisonment we read about at the end of the Acts. He then travelled again fairly extensively before being rearrested and brought back to

Rome. Apparently there was no dispute about that in the early church – it was taken as read that he was released and travelled again but in more modern times questions have arisen. One thing, however, we can be certain about is that his second imprisonment in Rome was entirely different from the first. At the end of the Acts of the Apostles, Luke gives us a picture of Paul living with a reasonable amount of freedom in his own hired home. That is not the case, of course, when Paul writes this letter. You see, in 1:16 he is chained. He repeats that again in 2:9 describing himself as 'chained like a criminal'.

I think you can understand his specific situation if you look at chapter 4:16 where Paul writes, 'At my first defence, no one came to my support.' The preliminary hearing had taken place in Rome and Paul is now awaiting the full trial. It is clear from his famous words in chapter 4:6–8 that he doesn't expect to be released. As he writes to Timothy he is quite sure death is now absolutely certain. But he doesn't expect to die immediately. He wants more clothes because winter is coming and in 4:21 he urges Timothy, 'Do your best to get here before winter.'

The tradition is that Paul was imprisoned in the Mamertine prison which has been described as consisting of two gloomy, underground cells – the place where Rome's vanquished enemies were imprisoned and normally died. William Hendriksen describes Paul as being in a dismal underground dungeon with a hole in the ceiling for light and air. It is from this prison cell that Paul writes to Timothy. He refers to him in 2:1 as 'my son'. As I read the letter, it almost seems that I have begun to read something I shouldn't. You wouldn't be at all surprised if this letter had been delivered in an envelope, and on the envelope in large letters were written PERSONAL AND CONFIDENTIAL. It is a very emotional, a very personal letter.

So as you think about this letter being written, please don't imagine Paul sitting at his desk with books around him, pouring over every word, polishing the first draft and then the second draft before he releases it – it wasn't like that at all. William Barclay, in his commentary, describes Paul striding up and down a little room pouring out a torrent of words while his secretary, who apparently could still visit him, races to keep up with him. Paul's emotions are running high. That is the image I want us to have in our minds as we study this little letter.

So why does he write this letter? It would seem that there are two basic reasons. First, he has a very simple request: 'Timothy, I want you beside me in my hour of need.' In 1:4 he writes, 'I long to see you'. As we have seen in 4:9, 'Do your best [Timothy] to come to me quickly'. Paul was convinced of the presence of Jesus with him in his hour of need. Commenting on the occasion of his first offence in 4:16–17 he writes, 'No one came to my support . . . everyone deserted me . . . But the Lord stood at my side and gave me strength'. There is no doubt in Paul's mind of the presence of Jesus as he faces death in that prison cell. But, equally, there is no doubt that the presence of friends at a time like this would be a huge encouragement. Great apostle he may be, but he is not some spiritual superman with no need of the help of anyone but Jesus. We need one another in the body of Christ – even the most experienced, apparently godly, members of the body, need encouragement from their brothers and sisters.

The second reason for the letter is a spiritual desertion which was causing the apostle great concern. He refers to this in chapter 1:15, 'You know that everyone in the province of Asia has deserted me'. Now this isn't the continent of Asia, it is the Roman province which consisted of the western part of Asia Minor with its capital at Ephesus. We can't be absolutely sure of what Paul is referring to here. The word translated 'everyone' is often used in the general sense; it doesn't necessarily mean total defection. Most likely it means that defections in Asia had been so staggering that even friends, such as Phygelus and Hermogenes, from whom Paul would have expected more, have deserted him. Paul is very concerned that Timothy stands firm in these enormously difficult days. And before he leaves Ephesus to come to Rome, Paul wants Timothy to take steps to ensure the believers will be strengthened and they too will stand firm.

Well, I hope that is sufficient background to give us a context for what we are studying this week. I want to place what I am going to say this morning under four headings. I want us to look at Paul's conviction, Paul's concern, Paul's confidence and finally Paul's strategy. I apologize for having four points and not three and I apologize that they don't all start with 'C' – you just can't get proper preachers these days, can you?

Let's look first at Paul's conviction. He introduces himself in verse 1 as 'an apostle of Christ Jesus by the will of God'. And I think it is very important to remember this as we seek to visualize Paul in this cell. How does Paul feel about his circumstances? You will notice that in verse 8, he urges Timothy not to be 'ashamed of me his [that is, Christ's] prisoner'. It is vital to understand that Paul does not see himself primarily as a prisoner of Rome. He sees himself as Christ's prisoner in Rome. He is there because he's fulfilling his divine calling. He is there because he is walking in obedience to the will of God and if walking in obedience to the will of God leads to prison, then so be it. Living in the will of God, fulfilling his apostolic calling, had led to what the majority of people in the world would describe as one big mess. He is on death row, forsaken by the majority of his colleagues; there is a mass desertion from the faith. The very cause to which he has devoted his life seems to be on the brink of annihilation. It is an apparent waste. Could this supremely gifted and able guy not have come to a better end than this? And if prosperity and success by human standards are indeed the marks of a God-blessed life, then this apostle was singularly unblessed. But we all know the famous words of chapter 4 and the total sense of satisfaction which Paul expresses in these circumstances: 'I have fought the good fight, I have finished the race, I have kept the faith' (v.7). The visible results of his ministry must have been exceedingly discouraging but, nevertheless, Paul is convinced he is in the will of God, he is fulfilling his apostolic calling, and it has brought him peace and deep satisfaction even in the face of death.

But what is this about death? Look at the second half of verse 1: 'Paul, an apostle of Christ Jesus by the will of God, according to the promise of life that is in Christ Jesus'. Confined by the walls of the prison, facing imminent death, Paul's concentration is on the life that is in Christ Jesus. I ask myself, do I need to have everything right around me to really enjoy life? Do I need my home comforts? Do I need my health to be in good order, my future provided for to really live? Here is something quite different. His friends, all apart from Luke, have gone. He wants clothes brought to him because it is cold. He asks for books to be brought to him to battle the boredom, but his message is of the life that is in Christ Jesus.

And the theme of life can be traced throughout this letter from death row. Chapter 1:10: 'the appearing of our Saviour, Christ Jesus, who has destroyed death and has brought life and immortality to light through the gospel'. Chapter 2:11-12: 'If we died with him, we will also live with him; if we endure, we will also reign with him.' And, of course, famously in chapter 4:8, 'Now there is in store for me the crown of righteousness, which the Lord, the righteous Judge, will award to me on that day'.

Our message is the promise of life in Christ Jesus even in the most dire, dreadful circumstances. I wonder if you have read Naomi Reed's excellent book, *My Seventh Monsoon*. I highly recommend it. She describes a weekly Bible study in the leprosy hospital where she was working in Nepal.

> The leader was Chandra. He'd also been a victim of leprosy . . . One Tuesday morning he said, 'Today we're going to read from a book at the end of the Bible . . . and this is what it says . . . "Then I saw a new heaven and a new earth, for the first heaven and the first earth had passed away, and there was no longer any sea. I saw the Holy City, the new Jerusalem, coming down out of heaven from God, prepared as a bride beautifully dressed for her husband. And I heard a loud voice from the throne saying, 'Now the dwelling of God is with men, and he will live with them. They will be his people, and God himself will be with them and be their God. He will wipe every tear from their eyes. There will be no more death or mourning or crying or pain, for the old order of things has passed away.' "'
>
> There was quiet in the room for a while and some of the patients started slowly raising their stumps of hands and staring at them. Others looked down at their feet, which were so deformed, covered with ulcers and open sores. They started to cry. All they'd ever known was that they were nothing, they were the outcasts, the untouchables – they didn't even deserve food. And now suddenly this – hope for an eternity with God where there would be no more tears. And then they held their hands even higher and it was as if they were trying to imagine being made new, with whole hands and restored feet. And more of them were crying and others were singing and I was as well . . . It was

perhaps one of the most moving Bible studies I'd ever been part of, and, for months afterwards, all I wanted to do was to read the Bible as they read it, to imagine what that would mean.[1]

In a congregation of this size I am sure there are people facing huge trials. Over the last twelve months we have been facing the most difficult period of our family life. Sometimes we felt the weight of the trial so great it seemed it might break us. Our Lord's words to Simon Peter have come to mind over and over again: 'Satan has asked to sift you as wheat. But I have prayed for you, Simon, that your faith may not fail' (Luke 22:31–32). How crucial, when our faith is being sifted, to know as Paul knew, we are in the will of God and the promise of life in Christ is ours, however dire the circumstances. There is no safer place in the storm than in the will of God, putting our trust in the promise of life, the life of the Spirit today and the assurance of eternal life – it is a promise no opposition can rob us of. So there is Paul's conviction – I am an apostle by the will of God. Even though I am facing death I speak to you about the promised life in Christ Jesus.

Let's look secondly at Paul's concern. As we have seen, the gospel was under significant attack. We have already noted the statement in chapter 1:15, 'everyone in the province of Asia has deserted me'. Bishop Handley Moule commented that to everyone except believers it must have seemed as if the gospel was on the edge of extinction. And this is Paul's concern. I am not sure it would have been my concern in his circumstances. I fear my chief concern might have been fighting for my life, defending myself, concern for my comforts and survival. But defending the gospel seems to be a far greater concern for the apostle and we notice this throughout the book – chapter 1:8: 'join with me in suffering for the gospel', right through to 4:2: 'Preach the word', to 4:5: 'endure hardship, do the work of an evangelist'. What a challenge this man is. He is a human being just like us. He is facing death, he has been deserted, he is struggling with his own life in prison but his chief concern is for the gospel that so transformed his life that day

---

[1] Naomi Reed, *My Seventh Monsoon* (Milton Keynes: Authentic Media, 2011), pp. 53–54.

just outside Damascus. His concern is for the preservation and the proclamation of the gospel and that is not going to change even now as dark clouds are gathering all around him.

Let's look thirdly at Paul's confidence. When he encourages Timothy in 1:8, 'join with me in suffering for the gospel,' he immediately adds, 'by the power of God'. When he writes in 2:9 about being chained like a criminal he immediately adds, 'But God's word is not chained.' Surrounded by so many challenges and trials in this cell Paul knows that the work, the preservation of the gospel, is not dependent on him. It is not dependent on his ability or on his strength. It is dependent on the power of God – yes, he has a part to play, a significant part – but he knows that he can only play his part by the power of the Holy Spirit. And he is convinced, because of the availability of the power of God, that ultimate victory is assured, even when the odds appear to be totally stacked against him. When, to every eye but the eye of faith, the gospel seems on the eve of extinction, he knows that extinction will not be the result. And we now have 2,000 years of remarkable testimony to support that. Every attempt has been made to extinguish the light of the gospel. Servants of the gospel have been locked up and murdered, Bibles burned, critics of the Bible have sought to deny its truth, but today the fruits of the gospel are more evident around the world than at any other time in history.

Probably the last place you would expect the growth of the Christian church today is Iran. But do you know that more people have come to know Jesus Christ in the last thirty-one years in Iran than in the previous 1,400 years? What is your conviction about the power of God? What is your confidence as you struggle in a personal or ministry situation? Paul's confidence is in the power of God.

Finally, move with me to Paul's strategy. How does he take steps to ensure the preservation and continuing proclamation of the gospel – how does he do it? I think it is important to recognize that he did take steps. He knew the gospel would only be preserved and proclaimed by the power of God – he knew that power was operative – but he still took definite, practical steps. He didn't just pray about it. The most important step he took was to invest in people. He particularly invested in the next generation. He knew that there was a day coming when he would no longer be able to do what he was doing. He would no longer be able to give the leadership he was giving and he ministered constantly with that in mind.

How many Christian leaders fail at this point? They lead with great enthusiasm but when they can no longer do what they are doing the ministry falls apart or it goes through a huge crisis, losing valuable momentum because transition preparations have never been considered. It happens over and over again. There can be a number of reasons for it: sometimes we can be so busy with the present that we give no time for tomorrow; it's just another example of the *urgent* crowding out the *important*. However, I think we have to say that often this can be due to a character flaw in some leaders. I call it 'insecure leadership' and it is so destructive of God-glorifying leadership. It happens when your position becomes confused with your identity. Your self-worth is wrapped up in your position. Who am I? I am the International Director of Operation Mobilization. No, no, no! That is my job at the moment but it is not who I am. When your job and your self-worth get wrapped up in each other then any thought of losing your job, well, it can't be countenanced, can it? So a younger person comes along with the leadership gifts to take over from you one day. That person is not considered to be a gift from God to you; that person is considered a threat you must deal with. And this can lead to abusive leadership where the leader begins to deal badly with that person to try and remove the threat. I have had to deal with a number of situations like this. I have written a bit about it if you are particularly interested. One thing I have discovered is nine times out of ten, Christian leaders involved in this sort of abusive leadership have no idea they are doing it. When they are approached about it they are shocked that anyone would consider they behave in this way. They genuinely can't see that they are doing it and this, of course, makes the problem even more difficult to deal with.

I love the way Paul takes his divine calling as an apostle and leader with the greatest seriousness, but I equally love the way he holds that position with open hands rather than clasped, closed hands. Remember, when he writes to the Corinthians describing the church as a building in 1 Corinthians 3:10 he says, 'By the grace God has given me, I laid a foundation as an expert builder, and someone else is building on it. But each one should be careful how he builds.' Paul knew what his calling was. He knew what his gifting was. He was committed to giving his contribution then perfectly content to move on and for others to move in.

So we will see Paul investing in Timothy but, while this is his most important ministry relationship, it is by no means the only important ministry relationship. In the last chapter of the epistle, Paul mentions sixteen other individuals he had been working with, or he was still working with. The last chapter of Romans is quite remarkable – Paul mentions thirty-three names of people who he is involved with. Paul has his eye on the future. He is ready to invest in people. He does not see these people as a threat but as the way forward to proclaim and preserve the great gospel of the Lord Jesus.

So let's have a look in the last five minutes at the Paul/Timothy relationship, so vital to both men. Two things in particular come to Paul's mind as he thinks of Timothy. First of all, the last time they parted Paul recalls tears were shed (1:4), probably referring to the time when Paul asked Timothy to stay at Ephesus to deal with the false teachers. So Paul was leaving him in a very difficult situation. Also, Timothy knew that as Paul left he was in considerable danger and, of course, his arrest and imprisonment in Rome followed. Then, secondly, Paul remembers Timothy's 'sincere faith' (1:5) – a word which can also be translated 'faithfulness'. So as we'll see over the next few mornings Paul investing in Timothy, we will see the making of a young man of God. We will see the evidence of Paul's commitment to the preservation and continuing proclamation of the faith.

I just want to take time to look at the first influence in the spiritual forming of this young man. This genuine faith in Timothy, Paul writes first, 'lived in your grandmother Lois and in your mother Eunice' (1:5). There is a strong emphasis in these verses on the continuity of the faith. Paul seems to be saying, 'Come on, Timothy, press on with me. The way may be hard but don't be discouraged, this faith has a long history. Many battles along the way but here we are still alive and well.'

It is immensely challenging but deeply humbling to remember where we stand in Christian history, to remember those who have gone before us, many of whom have paid a great price – and some the ultimate price – that the gospel might be preserved for us today. I have already mentioned Paul's words, 'Be careful how you build on the foundation laid.' So, think for a moment of the foundation laid in your local church over the years. Think of the foundations laid in your own life, possibly by your parents or someone who prayed and worked on your behalf. It is a great responsibility to build on the foundation laid. But it is also an enormous privilege. We have a part to play in con- tributing to this great building that brothers and sisters have been adding to over the centuries. God is building his church and we are privileged to be labourers together with him.

Building on this wonderful heritage, we must do so in such a way that we guarantee the future. The primary way to do that is through our families. We have been thinking about *Word to the World* – mission in the church, mission from the church, but the home is a vital sphere of mission - crucial, I would suggest – to the preservation and the development of our faith. But what is the dominance of television, video games and the internet doing to mission in the home? With the loss of family devotions in so many Christian homes, the loss of qual- ity time between parents and children, what is happening in this vital area to the passing of faith from generation to generation?

So here is the first influence in this young man's life - his family. I have run out of time so we will look at others tomorrow morning. I am excited by the epistle and I trust I can pass on some of the excite- ment to you.

The Lectures

Is it worth it?

by Helen Roseveare

Helen Roseveare

Helen Roseveare was born in England in September 1925, and born again as a first-year medical student in Cambridge University in 1945. She joined WEC International missionary society in 1952, sailing for the then Belgian Congo in 1953 where she served as a medical missionary for twenty years. Since returning to the UK in 1973, she has served on the home-end of WEC, challenging young people, university students, church youth groups, and women's groups, to consider God's claims on their lives for full-time service.

Is it worth it?

I think this is my seventh or eighth time of coming to Keswick. I've always been where you are. I'm telling you, it's pretty awesome to be up here looking at you instead of the other way round! When Jonathan wrote and invited me to come to Keswick and be this side, and not your side, I was horrified! I just felt, 'It's not me.' In the letter, he said there were two things he wanted me to do; one of them was to give the Keswick lecture. I nearly curled up and died! I don't give lectures. And then he added, 'What we want is your testimony.' I thought, 'I can cope with that.' I do know how wonderfully the lovely Lord Jesus has kept, guided, and supported me. He has brought me through some exciting adventures, some horrific situations, and he's always the same. When others hear what I say they don't think, 'I could never do that.' They just say, 'If he did it for her, he can do it for anyone!'

Now, I've often been asked, particularly as I look back over the missionary years in Congo, 'Was it really worth it? Is it really worth having Jesus, not just as one priority, but as *the* priority over all, over everything?' And I say, 'Yes, 100 per cent.'

My mother tells me I grew up asking the question, 'Is it worth it?' I remember as a teenager being told I had to learn Latin. And I thought that was the most stupid thing I'd ever heard! What was the point in learning Latin. Nobody spoke it; it was a dead language. But they said, 'If you don't, you won't be able to go up to University.' So it *was* worth it. I made the effort, I learnt Latin and I actually passed the exam – and the day after the exam I forgot everything!

Then I went to university to train to be a doctor and I had a seven-year course lying ahead of me. Friends who had been at school with me had finished their three-year courses, got their degrees and were out working, getting a salary and having summer holidays. I was slogging away for seven years and the question came, 'Is it worth it?' But there was a goal and that goal made it worth sticking to the task.

When I went up to university I was not a Christian; I was a church-goer. World War II was still on and the first big decision to make was, 'Do I really believe there is a God?' God seemed very irrelevant. He wasn't able to stop the war. Like many others we had family members in the war, some of whom never came back. Why didn't God stop it? If God was all-powerful, why didn't he step in and control this crazy situation? And yet, I hadn't quite the courage to say, 'I don't believe in God.' If you didn't believe in God, you had no one left to say what was right or wrong, no standards left. And my mind could quickly see that this would be utter chaos; even in very simple things we need someone who sets the standards for what's right and what's wrong.

During this searching period I met some girls in the Christian Union. I began to see that there was something different in these girls. They were always the same; there was a generosity and a kindness about them that was quite exceptional. I began to feel, 'I want to know what they've got.'

One day I asked them, 'Where do you all go after supper?' And they said, 'We have a prayer meeting.' Well, I hadn't a clue what a prayer meeting was but I said, 'Well, can I come?' So my first introduction to true Christianity was going to a prayer meeting! Listening to them praying it was obvious they knew the person they were speaking to. This, to me, was totally revolutionary. I never thought anybody really knew God. A desire began to grow in me but then there came the question, 'Is it worth it? Is it worth believing as they believed?' I knew if I became one of them a lot of things would have to change: my language, the books I chose to read, where I went in off-duty times. There was something different about these girls but would it be worth losing all that I knew at the present time? Afterwards, I wondered how

I could ever ask, 'Is it worth knowing Jesus?' But I didn't realize that at first.

They organized for me to go to a Christian house party, my first Christmas up at University. They were all Christians, except me. They all knew I wasn't and I thought I was. But I didn't really stand a chance because they were all praying for me! During that house party I heard Bible studies given by Dr Graham Scroggie on Genesis and Romans. I heard the gospel message put in a way I'd never heard before and my hunger grew.

On the last day something was said at the supper table and I lost my temper. There was a sudden horrid silence. I felt ashamed and I rushed out of the room. I went up to the dormitory where I was sleeping and I threw myself on my bed. I was in tears and I said, 'God, if there is a God, please make yourself known to me now!' And I looked up through my tears and there, on the wall of the dormitory, was a verse of Scripture printed. But it had been raining and the roof had been leaking and no one had repaired it so the last word of the text had been wiped out. And I read, 'Be still, and know that I am . . .' The rain had wiped out the word 'God'. I was overwhelmed, God had answered – 'Be still and know that I am'. And suddenly – I can't explain what happened – light filled my heart and his love swept into me and over me. That night I fell in love with Jesus. And, by his grace and goodness, I've never fallen out of love with him; he's still the same lovely Lord Jesus.

When I went downstairs, they gave me a Bible with Philippians 3:10 written in it – 'I want to know Christ and the power of his resurrection and the fellowship of sharing in his sufferings, becoming like him in his death'. And Dr Scroggie looked at me and said, 'Tonight you started that verse, "that I may know Christ". It is my prayer for you in years to come that you will come to know more of the power of his resurrection.' And then, looking straight at me, very quietly he said, 'Maybe one day God will give you the privilege of sharing in the fellowship of his suffering.' I had been a Christian half an hour and here was this famous doctor telling me that it was a privilege to suffer for Jesus!

And when I went up to bed later that night I eventually found my way to Philippians 3 and read it. The chapter in our Bible doesn't actually name Paul, so I didn't know who had written this. I didn't know anything about him or his situation. But he wrote, 'whatever was to my profit I now consider loss for the sake of Christ. What is more, I consider everything a loss compared to the surpassing greatness of knowing Christ Jesus my Lord' (Phil. 3:7–8). As I read that passage I said, 'Lord, I want to love you like that man; I want to love you with every bit of myself; I want to hand over everything to you, that you will control, guide, lead, overrule.'

The first time I came to the Keswick Convention I remember asking God, 'God, if you ever found it in your will to do it, would you give me the privilege of being a missionary?' So I finished my medical training then I went to missionary training school. They told us that if you go out to the mission field single, you will stay single and I did – but is it worth it? Yes. And there were other things: they weren't offering us a pension or any particular salary; you wouldn't have a radio, a washing machine; you probably won't have electricity where you're going – did it matter? No. There was a sense of sheer joy, privilege and wonder of serving God wherever he sent me.

In 1953 I left for the Congo. When I arrived there I had to learn a new culture and a new language. I was the only doctor for half a million people, serving in an area about three times the size of the UK. And it overwhelms you, day after day, night after night. You were on duty eight days a week, fifty-three weeks a year, and it never stopped. I had no senior doctor to turn to so was endlessly looking in books to find what I should do for this, that, or the other. Then when I couldn't do what the book told me to do, I had to invent something else instead. Sometimes I did feel almost crushed by the responsibility and there might have been a moment when I asked, 'Is it really worth it?' You began to question slightly but then there were other things to get on with. There was no hospital – they told me they'd been praying for me for over thirty years but they hadn't bothered to build a hospital before I got there! So I had to learn to build a hospital. That meant learning to make bricks, burn bricks, and put bricks on bricks. I used to write home to my dear mother, always asking for a book, 'Mum, can you find one of those *teach yourself* series – teach yourself how to build a hospital in the middle of Africa!'

On one occasion I'd been up about thirty-six hours without a break. I was doing an emergency operation at about 11 o'clock at night and as I came out of the operating room, taking my gloves off, a nurse came in and said, 'There's a patient that's just been brought in, doctor.' I thought, 'No, no more, I've had it,' and he said, 'Doctor, they've walked for eight days.' And so, with gritted teeth, I went back and operated on him, but by now there was almost anger in my heart against God.

I went to the committee and I said, 'I need your prayers; I can't take any more.' And they said to me, 'Doctor,' they're always gracious the Africans, 'Doctor, when you're being a doctor and doing these things, do you realize what we're doing? Every day you're in the hospital, we follow you. When you've done a ward round, we go in and talk to the patients; when you've got outpatients, we're sitting there talking with those that need help. Do you know we're leading twelve, twenty, thirty people to the Lord every week? Do you know they wouldn't come if you weren't here?' So I had to learn to be a member of a team. I'd gone out to be a missionary; I wanted to preach and teach the gospel; my heart's burden was to share Jesus, and here I was just doing emergency surgery. But God had set up a team to do it and I had to learn my place.

On one occasion there'd been a new law passed by the government. Laws were passed by the government over the radio at 9 o'clock in the morning, but there was probably a thunderstorm and crackles on our radio so we hadn't heard it. And that day had been declared a public holiday, but I hadn't heard this and I was in college lecturing when the soldiers arrived. I was dragged out, hands tied behind my back, thrown up in a truck and driven off. I was taken to the prison; I was the only pale-skin in prison that day; I was the only woman in prison that day. And they made me strip off – just pants and a bra – and they took me out onto the front lawn to be jeered at by all the passers-by. I felt so ashamed. But God met with me, even in that situation. At midday the guards changed and a new guard came in and I was told I could go. He came up to me and said, 'Didn't you bring my wife's baby into the world last week?' I didn't know who he was and I certainly didn't know who his wife was, but I said, 'Oh, yes!' I was given back my clothes and was told I could go. You don't know how

God is going to work the situation out but he always does. And there were moments like that when I was tempted to say, 'Is it really worth it?'

Then we were taken captive by guerrilla soldiers during the civil war in the mid-sixties. It was horrific. Everyday I woke with fear, terrified of what was going to happen next. And yet through it, I called upon the name of Jesus and every time I said, 'Jesus,' peace came in. It didn't drive out my fear, it was there with it; it was just the way things were. During that time, they came into our village one day and they must have asked my house-lad or someone else who knew me well, what was my most precious possession. I was tied up outside in the courtyard and they were given my two manuscripts. I had worked on these two manuscripts in the twelve years I'd been in Africa. One was a medical textbook for my nursing students written in Swahili. And the other was a translation of Dr Graham Scroggie's book, *Know Your Bible*. I'd just completed the Old Testament section, from Genesis 1 to Malachi 4, and I had to watch them burn my two manuscripts. There were no copies; they were handwritten in an exercise book. And I suppose there were moments like that that if I'd said, 'Is it worth it?' there would have been a question mark – is it *really* worth it? Or is the price too high to pay?

Anyway, we were rescued and brought home to the UK. The opportunity arose to go back to Africa and we spent seven years reconstructing the college and rewriting new course materials for teaching. And then I was turned on by my own students. I think we were accused of embezzling funds but of course there were no funds; the only funds were free gifts that came to me from home and that I channelled into the work. But that didn't matter. Suddenly, I was not trusted by the people I had come to serve. It was harsh; it cut me. I remember going back home after the trial, picking up my Bible and saying, 'God, speak to me.' I was reading through the Bible in a year and I'd reached Jonah, so I read all through Jonah and it said nothing to me at all. I said, 'Lord, please speak to me.' So I read all through Jonah again and it still didn't speak to me. And I came back to Jonah chapter 1 for the third time and the Lord said, 'OK, you know Jonah chapter 1 – a great storm; who sent the storm? God. Why did he send the storm? To speak to Jonah. Who suffered by the storm? Everybody. Not only the sailors in that ship and all the cargo in that ship, but the sailors in all the other little ships that were around in the sea; there was a huge storm. Why? God wanted to speak to Jonah.'

We were in the middle of a huge storm. All the nurses had gone on strike; everyone was blaming me for their troubles. And God said, 'I'm trying to speak to you; why don't you listen?'

I said, 'God, I'm listening.'

He said, 'You told people before you went home after the rebellion, that Jesus was sufficient. You said whatever the situation, however hard it was, whatever happened, Jesus was enough, he was sufficient for every situation; don't you believe it?'

I said, 'God, of course I believe it.'

'No,' he said, 'You don't, not really. You want Jesus plus; you want Jesus plus recognition; you want Jesus plus a lovely film of pictures to take home to show people the wonderful job you've done.'

I said, 'OK, God, I don't want Jesus plus; I want Jesus and Jesus only.' And again he filled me with certainty that Jesus was sufficient, and 'Is it worth it?' Yes, yes, it was worth it, even the humiliation of that court scene.

In all his ways God is in control. You see, it's even worth it now. Over the last thirty-five to forty years, I've been living out of a suitcase, talking. For quite a long time I'd be sleeping in a different bed every night and every day I'd have to relate to a new group of people. Each day you had to forget yesterday's people in order to relate to today's people. It was very lonely work, because you were always moving on and so you never saw any results. There were times I began to feel, 'Lord, I'd really love to do something else.'

But God said, 'It's what I want you to do; it's what I've trained you for.' Sometimes I felt I was almost losing my vision for the mission field but God said, 'Just keep going, I haven't finished yet.'

I want to go back to the rebellion, when we were taken captive by these wicked men. It was a cruel and terrifying night. I felt desperately alone; I was one pale-skin among a whole gang of dark-skinned people. Amongst the dark-skinned people were my students who tried to protect me. One of them, Hugh, stepped between me and the guard who was pressing a pistol on my forehead. I don't know if it was loaded or not but we both thought it was. Hugh was being held by rebels out in the courtyard and was so horrified he broke loose from the soldiers and threw himself between me and the rebel who was trying to shoot me. He said, 'You touch her over my dead body!' And they kicked him around like a football and beat him up so badly that I didn't know until two years later he had survived.

In the middle of that night, 28 October, there was a moment I felt God wasn't relating to me. I thought, 'God, where are you?' I suppose I was thinking about the price I was being asked to pay and in my heart I had got to the point of saying 'No, I can't pay this, it's not worth it.' And then the Lord met with me. You probably won't share my experience but we've all got our own situations to deal with where we're almost overwhelmed by what's happening and we cry out, 'God, where are you? Can't you step in and handle it?' That's where I was at. And he stepped in; he met with me. I did not have a vision. I did not hear a voice, but I just knew God was there and he was big, bigger than all these rebel soldiers. He was in charge. He did know what was going on. It was almost as though he said to me, 'Twenty years ago you asked me for the privilege of being a missionary – this is it. Don't you want it?' 'No!' Clear and simple, and then he whispered to me, 'Can you thank me?' And I thought, 'No, I cannot thank you for this – it's all too horrible, it's too much, I can't handle it.' But then he said, 'Can you thank me for trusting you with this situation?' That was amazing. I've always thought of me trusting him, but the thought that he was trusting me was overwhelming. And in saying, 'Can you thank me for trusting you?' he was really saying, 'Yes, I could have prevented this. I could have taken you out of this. I could have stopped it happening but, I, the Almighty God, have a purpose bigger than you can see. I know what's going to happen tomorrow. I know where this is going to lead, and you don't.' It is as though God was saying, 'I've allowed this to happen because I thought you knew me by now and wouldn't kick back at me, wouldn't lash out. Can you thank me for trusting you with this situation even if I never tell you why?'

In that moment I said, 'God, if we're all killed no one will ever hear about what we've gone through so I don't see how this will help anybody else but, God, if you've got a purpose, thank you. Thank you for trusting me.' And in that moment of saying thank you I was immediately filled with a tremendous sense of awe and understanding of the peace of God. It wasn't joy but it was peace. You see, once you thank God you can't have any bitterness towards him; you can't be saying, 'God, stop it!' And he said to me, 'Instead of asking, "Is it worth it?" and looking at the price you think you have to pay, would you ask, "Am I worthy?"' And as soon as you say, 'Is he worthy?' you realize our amazing privilege – of course he's worthy! There's nothing he brings into our lives or allows to occur in our lives that he is not able to handle and cope with and he's entrusting it to you. A clay jar, easily brittle, easily breakable, often cracked, but indwelt by the most precious treasure, the lovely Lord Jesus. Even in those difficult moments he's there.

When we say, 'Thank you, God, for trusting me with this,' he whispers, 'Am I worthy?' And you say 'Yes, Lord, 100 per cent worthy.' And when we recognize the absolute worthiness of Jesus we realize the privilege we have of being the clay jar to carry him. Each of us is called by God and sent out to serve him. It doesn't matter how far he sends you – it might be to your next door neighbour. Distance has got nothing to do with it. We are called by God, we are sent out to serve him, we are commissioned, and there will be moments in all our lives when it's tough, it's hard going, and if you ask 'Is it worth it?' you'll be tempted to say, 'No.' But lift up your hearts and your eyes to Jesus, fix your eyes on him as Hebrews tells us, and you'll find that he'll never fail you, he'll never let you down, he is worthy (Heb. 12:2).

The Bible today: Its claim for all peoples and cultures

by Michael Nazir-Ali

Michael Nazir-Ali

Michael Nazir-Ali was the 106th Bishop of Rochester for 15 years from 1994. Holding both Pakistani and British citizenship, he assisted the Archbishop of Canterbury for the 1988 Lambeth Conference, became General Secretary of the Church Mission Society, and entered the House of Lords in 1999. He is now President of the Oxford Centre for Training, Research, Advocacy and Dialogue. He has written several books and numerous articles.

The Bible today: Its claim for all peoples and cultures

I want to begin with a phrase of Michael Green's. When he was commenting on the debates about the Bible and living the Christian life he wrote that it's a choice between revelation and speculation. And I thought at the time it sums up the question very well. Of course, there are some people who are into speculation. They are endlessly asking questions about the human condition; they are exploring all sorts of things like New Age, Buddhism or the power of positive thinking. You just have to go into any bookshop to see the shelves awash with this material. There is no end to speculation and, indeed, constant speculation about the nature of the Bible, its background and so forth. By contrast, I hope that all of us are people not of speculation but revelation. The starting point must be that we acknowledge that God has revealed himself in act, in word and in presence.

The question then is, 'What is the relationship of the Bible to this revelation of God?' And the best description I've come across was actually in an ecumenical agreement where it was said, 'The Scriptures are the inspired record of the foundations of faith.' Now, each of those words bears some reflection, but what it means in the first instance is that the Scriptures testify to how God has revealed himself to his people and how he has worked among them. They are a testimony, a

witness, and, of course, as we shall see later on, they are a reliable witness to all that God has said and done.

But I also want to draw your attention to that other word. It is not
just any record, it is not just any witness or testimony, it is an 'inspired'
record. That is to say, the Scriptures, in being witness to revelation, also
partake of the nature of revelation. They are themselves revelation.
They are not just any witness to it. The proof of this is that so often
when the Scripture writers refer to what God has said they often just
say, 'the Scriptures said'. Even in Romans 9 when Paul is speaking of
Pharaoh, he says, 'the Scripture says to Pharaoh' (v.17) as a circumlo-
cution for God. But really it means, 'God said to Pharaoh'. The
Scriptures, therefore, are not only witness to revelation but are revelation themselves. It is in that sense that we read them for our coming
to faith, for our living the faith, for correction, for encouragement and
all of those things, as you know.

The apostolic teaching is received, passed on and received again.
The process goes on all the time. I mean, in Keswick it's been going
on for well over a hundred years. But as that process is going on in the
company of believers, which is the church of God, we find that people notice things both old and new. It's like the householder that Jesus
was talking about who brings out of his treasure things both old and
new (Matt. 13:52). So throughout history it has been noticed that
people who are living under some kind of oppression, who are
enslaved, who are exploited by other people, often notice the story of
the Exodus in the Bible. Why should they not? It is, after all, a story
about an enslaved people who were told to make bricks without
straw. You know, I used to work with bonded labour in the brick
kilns, trying to help them to change a very difficult situation in which
generations have found themselves. Of course, they had straw to make
the bricks with but it was back-breaking work. But when they hear
the Exodus story it comes alive to them immediately. African-
Americans, in their spirituals, often celebrate the Exodus story as
God's liberation of his people from their bondage. It is natural that
they should notice that kind of thing.

What about what has been called the 'feminine genius' in reading
the Bible? I'm not talking about feminism here but women, I think,

on the whole, read the Bible differently from men. They see different things in it. Valerie, my wife, reads the Bible differently from the way in which I read it. I learn a great deal from her and she may, from time to time, learn something from me. A critical study of the Bible is also important, of course. I'm not saying hers is uncritical – I don't want to get into trouble over lunch! There are different ways of reading the Bible and people notice different things in the Bible. In my work in the Islamic world, for instance, I have noticed again and again, the Bible's emphasis on the Oneness of God. Christians have learnt, I think, in the last fifty years or so to talk rather loosely about the Trinity as if we believed in three Gods after all. The Bible is a very useful corrective: 'Hear, O Israel: the LORD our God, the LORD is one' (Deut. 6:4). As we read the Bible we find things other people may have neglected or that may have gone unnoticed.

But then there is a more difficult question, 'How do we relate new knowledge to the Bible?' We live in an age where new knowledge and sometimes alleged knowledge is exploding all over the place, exponentially growing in a way that it never has for any other generation. The question is, 'What does the Bible have to do with this?' Now, you will be able to think of many examples of new knowledge but just to give you two. One of the things that we have had to struggle with in the last 150 years or so is different theories about how forms of life have emerged and developed on this earth. People have to relate to this in their science classes, at university, they may have to relate to it in their professions. Of course, we must take this new knowledge, new approaches to knowledge, seriously. But what we can't do is to allow this knowledge to control revelation. Rather it should be the other way round. It is revelation that controls – or should control – our approach to this new knowledge. For instance, if a theory about the development of different forms of life on this earth tells us or implies that there can be no purpose to the universe, that our lives are without meaning and destiny, that we cannot exercise our freedom or we have no freedom, then we must reject that claim of alleged new knowledge because we know from revelation that it is not true. Our lives do have meaning and purpose. Within limits we do have freedom to respond to God and to the world around us, and the world has purpose and direction. So new knowledge should not and cannot compromise this basic orientation that revelation itself has given us.

For six years, for my sins, I was the chair of the Ethics and Law Committee of the Human Fertilization and Embryology Authority (HFEA). In those six years I realized that there is now so much new knowledge about the early embryo, knowledge that even our parents could not hope to have had and certainly no other generations did. So we know a great deal about what happens at the early stages of fertilization, of implantation, of how the embryo develops into a foetus, and the foetus into a child. But, of course, the question is for us as Christians, 'What has this to do with the Bible's teaching about the dignity of the human person at every stage of life?' If we did not have this knowledge it would allow us to do anything we liked with the early embryo, as indeed some people want us to do.

I was talking to a woman MP who has introduced some quite modest Bills in Parliament to reduce the time limit for abortions. She said a delegation from the church visited her and they said, 'Look, many of our congregation are liberal and we are not sure they will buy all that you are doing.' This MP, as far as I know, not a Christian herself said, 'Well, what about Psalm 139?' And you know what this delegation from the church told her? They said, 'But that's just poetry!' You see, that is a failure to engage revelation with new knowledge.

Now, as we engage revelation and, indeed, our own minds and hearts with this new knowledge, it has to be a principled engagement. And what should be the principles? Well, a number of things can be said. For instance, our engagement with this new knowledge will have to be such that the essence of the good news of Jesus Christ is conserved. That is to say, what the gospel has to say about the human condition is not compromised in any way. Secondly, the engagement itself has to be conservative. We cannot just toss aside the wisdom of past ages, particularly Christian wisdom. So it is not just a matter of revelation but also how people have, down the ages, received that revelation. For example the testimony of the church in relation to the early embryo is unanimous that it cannot be manipulated or destroyed, simply for our benefit. And then there has to be continuity of principles.

How the church has always responded to situations of a similar kind has to be taken into account when we are dealing with new knowledge and anticipating what might happen in the next ten, twenty or fifty years. I was very conscious of this in the HFEA where there were scientific developments galore. Every week produced a major new scientific advance pressing us to do something more in terms of manipulation of the embryo. So, in developing a Christian response, it cannot just be about the presenting question but also anticipating what might arise, what might be around the corner.

When a question arises as to whether something that we are doing or thinking or writing is in accordance with revelation, how is that to be settled? In the Anglican Church we have been presented with this problem about human sexuality and what is permissible in terms of sexual behaviour. How is that kind of question to be settled? What is its relation to revelation? It is here that the Bible becomes the norm for deciding what is and is not authentically part of apostolic teaching. Now, the Bible is not only a norm, the Bible is to be read in devotion. We sing the Bible, we pray the Bible, there are many different uses of the Bible. But in this context when the question arises about Christian living, Christian behaviour, Christian believing, the Bible becomes the norm for what the church does and teaches. In this sense of being a norm, there are three things that were said about the Bible at the time of the Reformation, which are very important for us to remember.

The first is the clarity of the Scriptures. One of the marks of post-modernism is to say that no text bears a fixed meaning. You can read whatever you like into a text depending on who you are and what mood you are in at a particular time. Well, is that true? The text of the Bible certainly bears a definite meaning which has to do with our eternity, nothing less than that. Another quite common opinion found in post-modernism is that the intention of the authors cannot be known. Well, as far as the Bible is concerned, at least some of the authors have told us what their intention is. John wrote that these things were written so that you may believe and believing have life in Jesus, who is the Son of God (John 20:31). So when we speak of the clarity of the Bible we know that the text has a definite meaning, perhaps not fixed in the sense that different people might not notice different things in it, but it has a definite meaning. It cannot be made to mean anything at all, and at least in some cases we know the intention of the author.

Now, the clarity of the Scriptures is not unqualified. The clarity of the Scriptures pertains only to their significance for our eternal destiny, for our salvation. William Whitaker, the well-known Cambridge Puritan who debated for many years with theologians on the continent on this matter, recognized that there were obscure parts of Scripture, places where the meaning was not clear and scholars had to work very carefully to discover what the meaning was. What would biblical scholars do otherwise? But as far as salvation is concerned, the Scriptures are clear even to the ploughboy, as William Tyndale saw.

Secondly, the sufficiency of the Scriptures. Nothing can be required for us to believe as far as our salvation is concerned which is not in the Scriptures, or as Archbishop Whitgift said, 'which cannot be gathered from the Scriptures' or, as the articles of religion of the Church of England say, which cannot 'be proved thereby'. The Scriptures are not only clear but they are sufficient.

Thirdly, the supremacy of the Scriptures. Nothing can be set alongside Scripture in terms of authority. We live in a glorious Christian tradition, with a capital T if you like, that has gone on for two thousand years and we benefit from that tradition. But when a question arises within this living tradition of the church as to what is the apostolic faith, then it is the Scriptures that are supreme in determining for us what is the faith of the apostles and what is not.

Now, the point of all of this is to say that the study of the Scriptures is important. I mean, we study the Scriptures because they are absolutely vital for the personal life of a Christian but also, of course, for the life of the church as a whole. In this I want to point out one or two features of this study that I believe are important for our missionary journey.

The first is what you might call, 'studying what is behind the Scriptures'. That is to say, we are interested in how the Bible came into being as a collection of books. We are interested in the historical background, why the authors felt that something had to be written down, and the way in which the text has been edited and redacted down the ages. To be a biblical Christian does not mean to turn away from this kind of study. For Muslims the Koran is the directly revealed Word of God and so the historical background, the cultural affinities, dependence on other literature, is not important. But for Christians it is, because as Henry Martyn said when the Muslim Prime Minister of Iran asked him about the Bible, 'The sense is of God; the words are of men.' We are interested in what lies behind the Bible. We are interested in what is in the text because a careful study of the text enriches our knowledge of God's purpose for us.

Thirdly, it's not just what is behind the text and not what is in the text, but what is in front of the text. What is in front of the text? Well, it is the culture and contexts of the people round about. The Bible is brought into engagement in this missionary sense with people of all cultures, of all faiths, of all backgrounds, and of all languages. And it is this that lies at the heart of this project of translatability. Professor Lamin Sanneh, a prominent Christian scholar, initially researched how the translation of the Bible into different African languages has affected the culture. But he has gone on from this to research the nature of the Christian faith in its translatability. Sanneh points out that Islam is a worldwide faith present in many different countries and continents, but wherever it is found there is always a necessary 'Arabic-ness' there. The ritual prayer, the salat, always has to be said in Arabic, the call to prayer, the adhan, always has to be in Arabic. Although translations can be made, authoritatively the Koran is only in Arabic. But Sanneh says the Christian faith is not like this. The Bible has been translated into hundreds, thousands of languages and the Christian faith can be rendered into the terms, the language, the thought-forms, even the world views of many different cultures and peoples. Now, this is of central importance: when the Word of God comes to a culture it affects the culture, not just from outside, but changes it from the centre. The assumptions and presuppositions of a culture are challenged, sometimes affirmed, sometimes rejected and the culture is changed. But, of course, Christians also change. The Word of God does not change, but those who relate the Word of God from one culture to another change – ask any missionary. They begin to see how God's Word can change a culture in a way that people who have always lived in one culture can hardly imagine.

This importance of the Bible for culture is seen in our context in William Tyndale's translation of the Bible into English. It is quite difficult to imagine the English language developing the way it has without Tyndale. You can say almost that Tyndale, and later on, the King James Version of the Bible, has created the English language as we know it. Would the work of Shakespeare, Milton, George Herbert or John Donne have been possible without Tyndale? I really don't think so. So the translatability of the Bible has a great deal to do with the transformation of culture, and this we are seeing even today in many different parts of the world, in many different ways.

But there are also dangers in this process. The gospel can be made captive to a culture so that it can be seen to belong to one culture in such a way that other cultures think it's not for them. One of the great resistances to the gospel in the Islamic world is that Muslims – wrongly, of course, but nevertheless – see Christianity as a Western religion. And then sometimes – and we are living in such times – Christian people, Christian churches capitulate to the culture so the values of the culture that are contrary to the gospel and to the Bible determine what they believe about the Bible. This is one of the problems we are facing in what might be called liberal Protestant denominations – that the final authority of the Bible has now been replaced by the popular assumptions of our culture. Now, in this situation what can we say? On the one hand the engagement with culture is absolutely necessary, the gospel cannot be transmitted, cannot be accepted and lived without such an engagement. There is no argument about that. There is no dispute about it, but are there any limits to this engagement of revelation with culture.

I suggest that there are two limits which we need to keep in mind. First, whatever the engagement, wherever it may be, with whichever people, however long the church has been in existence in a particular country or culture, the engagement cannot compromise or negate the teaching of revelation. So if enculturation in any way affects fundamental teaching about the human condition, about God's plan for salvation, about the coming of Jesus Christ as God's eternal Word incarnate, about his sacrificial death for our sakes, his resurrection, the coming of the Holy Spirit - if any of this is compromised by the engagement with culture, then the engagement is not biblical. It's not faithful to revelation.

The second limit is the possibility of fellowship among Christians. I am from a background quite different from most of you but we are gathered around God's Word. We are people from different cultures, different backgrounds, different attainments, different achievements and failures. Nothing can be done in terms of our engagement with culture that jeopardizes the possibility of my fellowship with you, and your fellowship with me, or the fellowship of your church with my church, and of my church with yours. So, as people take the gospel to Africa or Africans bring the gospel to some part of this country, there's nothing that we should do that would jeopardize the fellowship between the churches in these two places. There was a time when I could go to an Anglican church in any part of the world and feel more or less at home, but I can't now, because the gospel has been compromised by capitulation to culture in one part or another. That has jeopardized the possibility of fellowship and this is tragic in an age when we can be in a completely different part of the world in a matter of hours.

At the time of the Reformation, there were two streams that emerged. There were those in the Roman Catholic Church, but also in orthodox churches, who emphasized the importance of the sacred ministers, those who had been commissioned in a line from the apostles to maintain the apostolic faith. Against this were mainly the churches of the Reformation who emphasized, not the sacred ministers, but the sacred deposit. What was authoritative for the church was not the line of ministers but this holy deposit of faith that is the Bible which is the inspired record of revelation. As a matter of fact, if you get beyond the controversy, both are necessary. The Bible itself teaches us that both are necessary. The sacred deposit is necessary for all the reasons that we have discussed this morning but there are also people – the Bible teaches this quite clearly – who are called to be teachers of the Word, to maintain the truth of the Word, to propagate God's revelation in the world. Of course, these teachers are not masters of the Word, they are its servants. Whatever calling we may have to bring God's truth and God's Word to people, we only do so as servants, and not as masters. But having said that, we need a good mix in the church of the authority of divine revelation as found in the Bible and the calling, the gifting, the commissioning of those who are to be teachers of that Word, who make sure that the church keeps faithful to the Word and who make sure that the church also takes the Word out into the world as your theme rightly emphasizes.

We live in a time when the Bible is more universal in its hearing, its receiving, and its reading than at any other time in history. But all of this will have been in vain if we abandon the supremacy of the Bible and accept without thought the importance of cultural assumptions and presuppositions. Now is the time to strongly affirm the authority of God's Word, not only for Christian believing, but for Christian living and for the missionary task of the church in our age and in every culture.

How the West was won (and might be again)

by Richard Tiplady

Richard Tiplady

Richard Tiplady is Principal of International Christian College in Glasgow, having previously served as British Director of European Christian Mission and Associate Director of Global Connections. He has also worked as a consultant for a number of Christian organizations including Tearfund. Richard is married to Irene and they have one son, Jamie.

How the West was won (and might be again): Acts 17

J.R.R. Tolkien, the well-known writer of *Lord of the Rings*, was a Christian and there is an enormous amount of theology in his writing. In the first *Lord of the Rings* film Frodo says, 'I wish we did not live in times like this', and Gandalf gives very wise words: 'It's not for us to choose the times we live in, but it is for us to decide how we live in the times that we are given.'[1] I think that's a very insightful comment. These are the days that the Lord has given us. These are the days that we have to serve him in. And these are different days – the days that we face are new and the challenges we face for the gospel are new.

I want to use the framework of Paul's speech to the philosophers on Mars Hill at the Areopagus. In Acts 17 Paul is at the centre of the philosophical world, the educated world. He's where the clever people are. He's speaking to educated pagans, and if educated pagans don't describe the people we live among in the UK today, I don't know what does. And so it seems to me that Paul's message here in Athens has particular relevance to us. The first thing I want to say about Paul and our situation is that to begin with he is a bit of a failure. Luke tells us he's there in the synagogue; he's also in the market place. He's excited about

---

[1] *Lord of the Rings: The Fellowship of the Ring* © 2001 New Line Cinema.

the meeting he's had with the risen Jesus and that's what's driving him. He's doing what apostles do: he's just sharing the gospel, but he's not very successful. The people listening are saying, 'What is this babbler trying to say? He seems to be advocating foreign gods.' Paul's a failure. He's not connecting; the message he is preaching is not making any sense whatsoever and that does reflect our situation today.

The culture despises Christianity in our day. The new atheists – Philip Pullman, Richard Dawkins, Christopher Hitchens, Terry Pratchett and Stephen Fry – think we're not even worth engaging with. Richard Dawkins notoriously refused to debate with a Christian for years. He said, 'Why would I waste my time? They are not even worth the effort.' It's a despicable attitude but that's how we, and even the very best of our thinkers, were seen by him – just as a waste of space, babblers, talking nonsense, not worth expending fresh air on.

This perception that the church is shrinking in the West is a story that has been told for the last forty or fifty years across Europe. It's called the secularization thesis: as societies modernize they get wealthier, they secularize and the place of religion becomes less important. And we bought into that; we tell that story to ourselves. We give in intellectually and emotionally. We say, yes, the church is shrinking, we're just hanging on, and things are getting worse. We tell ourselves a great number of stories that depress us, that in the end make us feel a little bit beleaguered, and a bit of a minority. We tell ourselves the stories of Christians who have suffered for their faith even in the West: Nadia Eweida, the British Airways staff member who wasn't allowed to wear a cross; Colin Atkinson, the employee of Wakefield Housing Association who couldn't show the palm cross in his van; Eunice and Owen Johns in Derby who wanted to get a legal ruling that as Christians they would be allowed to foster and tell the children that they were fostering that homosexuality was wrong, and the Judge says, 'No, you are not allowed to impose your views on others.'

We feel ourselves being pushed onto the margins but maybe that's just life. Maybe that's just something we need to deal with. Christianity has had a privileged place in our culture and we do not have that privileged place any more. But rather than trying to hang onto the past and hankering back to a lost time that maybe didn't exist anyway, perhaps it's time to say, 'OK, these are the times that God has given us.' Minority status is the norm for Christians round the world, and throughout most of history that has been the case. It was cert-ainly the case for Paul; it was the case for Christians in the first few centuries and yet it didn't stop the church exploding, not just over the Roman Empire but across the Persian Empire. By the time that the very first Roman and Celtic missionaries were evangelizing England in the sixth and seventh century AD, the church in China was so big it had an Archbishop. The church exploded across the world from a position of weakness, persecution and suffering, not of power.

Evangelical Christianity, the form of the faith that I think is bibli-cal and reflects the tradition we represent, flourishes not where it is in control but where there is freedom to think differently. Evangelicals have a very strong tradition of arguing for freedom of religion. When the Evangelical Alliance was formed in London in 1846, the very first thing it spent its time doing was not unity of evangelicals, but argu-ing for the freedom of belief. It was arguing that people should be free to believe what they want, and that includes those who don't agree with us. Martin Spence, until recently a lecturer in Church History at ICC, has commented that evangelicalism gives people the choice to embrace religious faith or unbelief. Choosing Christ, what we want people to do, also allows them not to choose him. We need to live with that. We need to be comfortable with that; we want people to be free to believe the gospel, and we have to take the risk that they will be free to choose not to.

Early evangelicals a couple of hundred years ago also had a very strong sense of starting again, of breaking away from the past, that God was doing something new in their day. Evangelical Christianity actu-ally contributed to the demise of Christendom. We protested against the uniformity of Christendom in a drive for true personal belief. By definition evangelical Christianity encourages experimentation. It encourages innovation; it encourages new things because of our indi-vidualistic emphasis on personal faith, on our direct access to the Father through the Spirit and, therefore, God being able to speak to us and start new things. Keswick was once the upstart, Keswick was once the new kid on the block. It's been going for well over a hundred years

– an incredible legacy – but at some point someone had to say, 'I know, let's do something wild; let's put a tent up in the vicarage garden and get Christians along to hear the Bible.' Amazing! Hankering back after some mythical past or even hanging on to what we've got is not honouring to God. It's not honouring to the gospel and it's not how evangelical Christians work. It's not what we do.

If we feel ourselves to be marginalized, if we are feeling in a minority, if we are feeling like things are tough and we are wondering where God is, then we have enormous biblical resources to help us. Go back to the Old Testament: the exile that Israel or Judah experienced in the 6th century BC was a time of profound loss. It was an enormous shock to the people because God had promised that his presence would be in the temple in Jerusalem and he would protect them. And what had happened? God had not protected them. Prophets arose to say, 'Don't worry, God has not abandoned us.' In Jeremiah 28 Hananiah says within two years the King, everyone else, and all the temple artefacts will be brought back. But in chapter 29 Jeremiah denounces Hananiah and says, stay where you are, 'build houses and settle down; plant gardens and eat what they produce . . . seek the peace and prosperity of the city to which I have carried you into exile' (29:5,7). The exilic literature says to us what Jeremiah says here, 'Don't listen to the false prophets who say everything's going to be OK. Start to seek the prosperity of the place that I have taken you to.' Or to quote Gandalf again, 'Deal with the times you've been given; don't hanker after the past.'

In the sort of communities, the sort of world, the sort of society we live in where people are free to choose, the groups that flourish are those of strong, freely chosen beliefs. Evangelicals across Europe are growing. In post-modern Europe, when people are free to believe, they choose things that are worth believing in. And have we got something worth believing? Of course we have! There are other groups that are also growing but, my goodness, if we can't say we have something worth believing then I don't know what we are doing here. So we need to have hope. God has not abandoned us but the times we live in are different.

Now, I don't want to become complacent. I don't want to pretend that everything in the garden is rosy. We need to be turning outwards.

There are, to my mind, some major challenges. I want to name two before going on to look at how Paul responded to the situation he faced in Athens. The first challenge is the large city churches and the small village churches. The churches that are growing in the UK tend to be in cities or larger towns. They can run big programmes, families can come along and know their children are going to be looked after, there's a good youth ministry, they've got amazing ministry out into the community, and they run strong evangelistic programmes. We used to go to an Anglican church down in the south of England called St Andrew's Chorleywood. In the previous six years it had grown from 800 to 1,600 people and the last Alpha course that we heard about had 147 people attending it. I remembered that because it's the top score in snooker! But that's fantastic, isn't it? That's amazing!

In Scotland the experience I observe is that in the cities the churches seem to be OK but the smaller churches in the towns and villages are finding it hard. Congregations are shrinking and churches are closing. Are we just going to be a city-based faith? Can our large churches be resource centres for the difficult places? I think it's something those of us who have the privilege of being in bigger churches have to take very seriously. Central Baptist Church in Dundee is a large church with 300 members. They've just planted a new church in Carnoustie, a small town along the coast where things were struggling, and they have basically given thirty to forty of their members to be the nucleus of a new church plant. City Church is a large 500-member church in Aberdeen. They are training younger leaders to be church planters in Scotland. They are giving away their best leaders to go to the tough places in our own country. That is a trend we need to take seriously and those of us who have the privilege of being in lar-ger churches have a duty to respond.

And the second, very serious, issue is the missing generation in our churches. The under thirties, or possibly even the under thirty-fives, are noticeable by their absence. We have made an incredible investment in youth ministry over the last fifteen to twenty years. What's gone wrong? Krish Kandiah and I had a coffee last week. He made the observation that perhaps we have created a church that is sort of consumerist. It certainly hasn't encouraged the transition of people from youth churches into what we might think of as mainstream church. The churches that have held on to their young people are those that keep them in *normal* church – we can debate that term! But this is a challenge for many of us because we are investing huge amounts and something is going wrong.

So that's the day that we live in and I think it has a lot of similarities to the day that Paul was living in. I said at the start that in the beginning Paul was a bit of a failure. He didn't connect. They sneered at him; they called him a babbler, and they just really didn't understand what was going on. But Paul's response to being rejected – Paul's response to indifference – was not anger, it was not blame. He was not confrontational; he was not negative. In fact, he was incredibly friendly towards them. In verses 22–28, he gives a speech. The start of his speech is remarkably positive, remarkably friendly, remarkably affirming of his hearers. He doesn't blame them; he doesn't accuse them, and he doesn't say they were wrong. He finds an enormous amount of common ground with them.

Anton Wessels is a Dutch Theologian who wrote a book with the fantastic title, *Europe: Was it ever really Christian?* In the book he talks about this passage and says that Paul claims for the Christian God the space left by the unknown god. And Wessels says that we need to look for the God spaces in our culture. We need to be looking for the places where God is working ahead of us because he has not abandoned our world, he has not abandoned our society, and he has not abandoned our culture. If the book of Acts tells us anything, it is that the Holy Spirit goes ahead of us. Acts 8–11 is the story of the expansion of the church after the martyrdom of Stephen. Stephen is martyred, most of the Christians scatter and as they go they cannot seem to help themselves; they just seem to share their faith. So Philip goes up to Samaria to the despised Samaritans and they respond to the gospel. Now, that causes a bit of consternation back in Jerusalem and Peter and John are sent to check things out. The two heavy guys go up to check things out, they pray and lay hands on, and the Holy Spirit comes, but the church was responding to what the Holy Spirit was doing. Peter himself went to talk to a Roman Centurion but not without a vision from God of that picnic in a blanket coming down from the skies. There's no other way he would have gone, but he realizes that God is going ahead of him.

Where are the God spaces in our culture? Where has God gone ahead of us, where is he preparing the ground for us? Let's not see the world out there as our enemy. Let's look for the places God is already at work and join him there because that's how God works. Let me give you three suggestions, the three that matter to me. Perhaps they are important:

Here's a quote that takes a little bit of unpacking, 'the collapse of the post-war welfare settlement'. This is a term in a book called *Postwar* by Tony Judt. What Judt means by this is after World War II the people of Europe said, 'We did not go through this conflict, this suffering, for nothing.' And across Europe different types of welfare states were established; that's why the NHS was established. But what Judt points out is that across the whole of Europe that has proved too expensive. Our political debates today are filled with discussions about how we can afford care for the elderly, NHS reforms, how can we reduce the unemployment, how we can afford the 1.5 million people on incapacity benefit. The welfare state in every European country is just too expensive; they are collapsing. But we as churches have really begun to get involved in this, haven't we? Over the last fifteen years, churches have been welcomed into the fold and increasingly we are involved in the delivery of social care of various types. David Cameron talks about *The Big Society* and Philip Blond, who is the philosophical inspiration of that, is a Christian. Churches are talking more and more about how we can be involved in serving our communities and supporting the vulnerable. Not saying, 'It's the State's job', but for Christians to reach out with the love of Christ, showing compassion and care. We have a huge opportunity here and it is incumbent upon us, I think, to reach out, touch and serve our nation.

Linked to our sense of marginalization, that I talked about earlier, it's interesting how often I hear Christians saying we need to be 'salt and light' in our society. I think what we are doing here is recognizing that we have lost the power, but we still need to be an influence for good. More recently we've heard people like Mark Greene of London School of Contemporary Christianity encouraging us to think about what we used to talk about as 'marketplace theology', now we talk about 'whole-life discipleship'. We recognize that the standards in our workplace, community and society might not be what we want them to be but, as Christians, we really want to be an influence for good. And I am so heartened by that. I think that's profoundly important and I am increasingly convinced that the work of the church and of pastors is exactly what it says in Ephesians 4:11–12: to equip the saints, to be Christians in the workplace and an influence for Christ in our communities. I think that's us responding already. I think it's the Spirit working among us responding to this perceived gap. I'm encouraged by it. I think it's a God space.

And the third thing that I think we have to take account of is the church is increasingly a bit like my hair, it hasn't got much of a fringe. This increasing demarcation between Christians and non-Christians, means that yes, there's clarification about who is a Christian and who isn't. And at one level I think that's really good. I'd rather someone said, 'I'm not a Christian', than pretended to be. I'd rather people realized they weren't Christians and have the opportunity to become one in the future. I don't think that's entirely a bad thing but that does mean that the fringe of churches, which is where most real conversions happen, is getting smaller. We need to be thinking about how we respond.

Twenty years ago, Robert Warren published a book called *Building Missionary Congregations*, and in it he said that missionary congregations will do fewer things. They will release their members from the programme to be involved in their communities to build relationships. Now, when I first became a Christian that wasn't the ethos. I went to an amazing Church and I'm so grateful for the youth group. It was incredible what God was doing, but the ethos of the church was that if you were a committed Christian then you showed up. It wasn't a joke. The minister of the church said once, 'What does the story of doubting Thomas tell us? Never miss a meeting. You don't know what might happen.' That was what discipleship was, it was being at the young adults' Bible study, twice at church on a Sunday, attending the nurture group and house group. My best friend became a Christian five weeks after me which was fantastic, and a few more came along to things. But within six months I'd lost contact with most of those friends. I was passionate about this new faith and, of course, I wanted to grow but we do need to be thinking about ways of being in our society, making sure we have friendships and relationships.

And church leaders, I want to say this to you, do not derive your self-worth from the number of people attending your meetings and the frequency by which they attend them, because all we do is decant ourselves and get ourselves away from the rest of the world. Let's derive our self-worth from seeing our church members serving Christ in our communities, their workplaces, being influences for good and then saying, 'By the way, we've got this *Alpha* course, we've got this *Christianity Explored* course, do you want to come along?' We have to take this seriously. This marginalization is separating us. How are we going to intentionally go out and find the places that God is working in?

Paul was enormously positive to his hearers, and I think we need to be enormously positive towards the society that we live in. That's all very well, but what about Jesus? What difference does Jesus Christ make? We get a hint in Paul's sermon that as much as he is being incredibly positive towards his listeners, he doesn't agree with everything. In verse 27 he says, 'though he is not far from each one of us'. The Greek philosophers thought God was enormously distant and Paul says, actually, he's very near and that prepares us for what he then goes on to do, which is to challenge and confront. He's been enormously positive. He's been very affirming, he's been very constructive, he has sought as much common ground as possible, but here comes the punch line. Here comes what really matters: he talks about repentance (v.30), turning away from idols. He talks about the God of justice and resurrection of Jesus from the dead (v.31).

Now, did you notice at the start that the reason that Paul was misunderstood was because he was talking about the resurrection (v.18). To his listeners, resurrection was not good news. Greek philosophy believed the human spirit was good but that the body was an evil material prison. The hope was that after death we would shed this material body and enter the realm of the spirit. The Greeks didn't want to hear about resurrection. That did not make sense, that didn't connect, that was bad news. But Paul as much as he's looking for common ground cannot compromise on who Jesus is, what God has done in Jesus Christ, and here he talks about the resurrection. It seems to me that whatever else we do – all the positive things we do, the way we try and connect, the way we try to be an influence for good, the way we show love and care for the vulnerable and the weak – the other thing that we can never, ever abandon is a simple commitment to evangelism. We need to recover our confidence in the gospel and be willing to be embarrassed, to keep going despite our embarrassment and keep finding ways of sharing our faith which, of course, requires us to have good relationships in order that we can do it. The resurrection was offensive. We will be offensive if we keep talking about Jesus. Let's be offensive in the right way.

A final thought is about this theme of resurrection. I said at the start that I think that this passage has a lot to teach us about reaching educated pagans, and that's a good way of describing the people we live and work with. Paul doesn't talk about the death of Jesus; he talks about the resurrection of Jesus. Now, I may be treading on dodgy ground here and I don't want to be misunderstood because as evangelicals we are cruciform – we are cross-shaped people. But here Paul is talking about resurrection, and I think that's important. Do you remember I said that the apostles shaped their message to their hearers' starting point? I don't think most people are wandering around the streets of Britain today worrying about their sins and how they can be forgiven. It might be true that they need to be but it's really not where they are. I became a Christian because of the offer of new life. That's what caught my attention, not sins forgiven; that's something I realized later. It was the fresh start, and if resurrection is not about fresh starts then I don't know what is. The resurrection of Jesus is saying that the world does not have to be the way it is, God has not abandoned it, he's committed to changing it, but we don't need to be the way we are. The cross on its own was catastrophe; it's the resurrection that brought meaning to the cross of Jesus. Jesus' physical resurrection and our physical resurrection say to the world God cares about this place: he made it, he wants to restore it, he wants to renew it, and he wants to renew us. What we do in this life matters. We are not just people of the cross; we are people of the resurrection. We have experienced new life in Jesus; we've experienced a fresh start because of Jesus Christ. That's the message of the gospel, that's the message that will transform our society, that will transform people and we will see Britain, Europe, the West, transformed again by the gospel.

The Seminars

A gospel church – its leadership

by Bill Bygroves

Bill Bygroves

Bill Bygroves is the Pastor of Bridge Chapel in Liverpool where he has served for more than 30 years. He is married to Dot and has four children and one grandchild. Bill enjoys all sports especially football and is the chaplain of Liverpool Football Club.

A gospel church – its leadership

Leadership is everything. Charlie was a church member but he came out of the members' meeting totally deflated. He'd expected unity in the church but there were divisions, suspicion and schism. He'd expected vision, direction, optimism, but he'd come out feeling lost. He'd expected warmth and love; he felt alone, rejected. As he was walking home utterly frustrated he saw an empty coke can. He kicked the can along the road thinking about all that had happened in the church meeting when suddenly something unusual happened. Whoops! Out of the can came the genie of the can! The genie can man! 'I am a junior genie. The senior genie practices in the lamp that you rub but I have been in the coca cola can. Remember, I am a junior genie and ask of me what you will.' Charlie the church member wondered, 'What's going on here?' He thought quickly. 'Please, please stop all the wars in the world; please stop all the famines in the world, and please heal all the marriages in the world.'

'Whoa,' said the junior genie, 'I just told you I'm a junior genie. I'm only learning my trade.'

'Oh, OK,' said Charlie the church member, 'well, could you make our pastor a leader?'

'Could we go back to the first one?' said the genie.

How sad that is! Leadership is everything.

This morning I have a number of things to say to you from the New Testament concerning leadership.

1. Leadership is vital

Leadership is not peripheral, it's not something secondary, it is primary. The world is crying out for leaders. Look at the business world, the world of commerce, the world of sport: they are crying out for leaders. Look at the political scene: it's crying out for leaders. And look at the church: it's crying out for godly, spiritual leaders. If you trace the history of redemption from Genesis to Revelation, you will find that the health or harm of the cause of God on this planet is tied up in leadership.

Come with me to the Old Testament, just for an illustration. Look at him as he walks into the room. All the ladies gasp; he is head and shoulders above everyone else in Israel. Tall, handsome, strong, robust, hey! He is Saul. If ever there was a leader anointed and appointed, he is the man. If ever there was a leader people want to get behind, he is the man. But he loves himself more than he loves God. The man or the woman who is wrapped up in himself has no place for God. Ultimately Saul is rejected. Then Sam the man comes to town and says to Jesse, 'One of your sons is going to be king.'

Out they come one by one and all the sons of Jesse are rejected.

Samuel is discouraged. He says to Jesse, 'Do you have any more boys?'

'Only him out in the field. You wouldn't be interested in him; I mean, look at him! And look at that sling, that catapult. He's a danger to everyone; he's better left out there!'

'Bring him in,' says Samuel.

In comes David and the brothers go, 'Oh, no,' and Jesse goes, 'Oh, no,' and even Samuel goes, 'Oh, no,' and God says, 'Oh, yes. That's my boy!'

He is the man after God's own heart. God says, I don't look on the outward appearance; I look upon the heart (1 Sam. 16:7). The heart of the issue of leadership is the issue of the heart: a consecrated, devoted heart in love with the King of Heaven. Leadership is vital. Listen to what Jesus said in Matthew 15:7-9, 'You hypocrites! Isaiah was right when he prophesied about you: "These people honour me with their lips, but their hearts are far from me. They worship me in vain;

their teachings are but rules taught by men."' Verse 14, 'Leave them; they are blind guides. If a blind man leads a blind man, both will fall into a pit.' Or read Matthew 23 – how horrendous to think that the King of Heaven and earth could pronounce woes, seven woes, upon respectable, religious leaders. 'You hypocrites, on the outside you are whitewashed, on the inside you are ugly, you look as if you are alive, but you are dead!' Leadership is vital; the health and the harm of the cause of the Kingdom depend on it.

2. Leadership is spiritual

Spiritual life is the prerequisite – leaders must know God. It is possible for a person to have a brilliant mind, a clean life, be articulate in word, courageous in deed, clear in vision, disciplined in habit, stable in life, sincere in heart, humorous in disposition, loyal in relationships. This person may be respectable, accountable, professional, able to stimulate, to articulate, to emulate, to motivate men and women. They may be able to cajole and encourage; they may be able to set and meet targets; they may be able to identify and then unify men and women to a common vision. They may be attractive in looks, stylish in dress, charismatic in personality, multi-talented in gifts, dynamic in presence. They may be able to gather a crowd, and people may be inspired by them. They may have the presence of Alexander the Great, the personality of J.F. Kennedy, the integrity of Abraham Lincoln, the audacity of Napoleon Bonaparte, the oratory of Winston Churchill, and still be disqualified from Christian leadership.

Nicodemus is a ruler of the Jews, a leader in his community. People look up to him; people go to him; he's a fount of knowledge. Ask him, does he believe God created the heavens and the earth? Yes. Does he believe the Old Testament Torah is inspired by heaven itself? Yes. Is he seeking to live a moral and godly upright life? Yes. But Jesus gets to the heart of the issue: Nicodemus, you need to be born again (John 3:3). The Wesley brothers were brought up in a Christian home, taught the Bible from childhood, went out to be missionaries and still didn't know God. They knew all about him, but they didn't know him. Not until the Holy Spirit strangely warms the heart, opens the eyes, unstops the ears, quickens the man, and brings him from death to life, from the kingdom of Satan unto God, does a person know God. The prerequisite of Christian leadership is that it must be spiritual leadership; the person must know God. They must be convicted of their sin by the Holy Spirit; they must be brought into newness of life by the Holy Spirit, and the Holy Spirit must bear witness with their spirit confirming that they are the children of God. Having the assurance of the Spirit they must be full of the Spirit; they must bear the fruit of the Spirit; they must keep in step with the Spirit because spiritual leadership is the issue.

In our churches – and even in some evangelical churches – it is quite possible that a person can look the real thing and never have been born again. Christian leaders, God's not interested in how many letters you have after your name. You can have more after your name than in your name. God's not interested if you wear a collar, or a tie, or an open-necked shirt or a gown. He's not interested in what seminary or theological training you went to, he's not. The only question he's interested in is, 'Have you been born again? Do you know God?'

3. Leadership must be credible

Please don't get me wrong. Please do not think as I speak through this list that the only people who are qualified for leadership are those who have never done anything wrong. Listen, the prerequisite for usefulness is brokenness. The Bible makes it plain the only people God can use are broken, fallen, wounded, vulnerable and sinful. Peter had blown it big style, but God can use those who blow it big style if they will humble themselves and return to him. Peter had been a fisherman, the son of the sea. You can picture him, can't you, tall and handsome, brown with tattoos all over his arm. He is the sort of person who puts his foot in it time and time again. But he's been humbled, and now under the inspiration of the Holy Spirit he's writing about Christian leadership. In 1 Peter 5:1–4 he says that leaders should be shepherds, those who lead the sheep, not beat the sheep; those who feed the sheep, not flog the sheep; those who are examples to the flock of God.

There is an integrity crisis in our world. Look at the phone-hacking scandal. There's an integrity crisis in the church and we need credible Christian leadership characterized firstly by character, secondly by competence and thirdly by chemistry. What do I mean by that? Well, there is no substitute for a godly character. When Paul wrote to Timothy in 1 Timothy 3, he laid down what the moral requirements were for a person to be in leadership. Character is vital; competence is vital. Is this man, this woman equipped? Are they gifted? Leadership is a spiritual gift, given from heaven. And do they have chemistry; do they love others? Do they lead others? We need credible Christian leadership.

4. Leadership must be humble

Leadership must be based on service, not status. I've got to be honest with you: it worries me how quickly people rush into ministry positions. Dr Lloyd Jones used to counsel his students never to rush into ministry; it's too huge a responsibility. What does James say? 'Let not many of you become teachers' (Jas 3:1, NKJV).

But we have men and women today who are arrogant and super-confident. They go to classes to learn how to assert their leadership. And up and down the country there are Christian men and women who are being bullied by their pastors! Pastors who say, 'Believe what I believe, no more, no less, that I am right and no one else confess. Say what I say, do what I do and then I might have fellowship with you!' How alien is that to New Testament leadership? If you are in a church where the pastor is authoritarian, leave! If you are in a church where the pastor is a bully, leave! The world, the flesh and the devil is enough without a bully as a pastor.

When asked what are the three qualities that make a man of God, Augustine said, 'Humility, humility, humility.' And humility has nothing at all to do with personality. Peter, who wrote in 1 Peter 5:6, 'Humble yourselves . . . under God's mighty hand,' was a larger than life personality but he had been humbled. He knew what it was to 'act justly and to love mercy and to walk humbly with your God' (Micah 6:8). Humility has nothing to do with whether you are an introvert or an extrovert; it has to do with your spirit. How many people do you meet who are as quiet as a church mouse; they wouldn't say boo to a goose! But inside they are like volcanoes waiting to erupt. Say something wrong to them and they will hold it against you for the rest of your life. Humility has nothing to do with personality; it's to do with spirituality; it's to do with acknowledging, 'Lord I am nothing; Lord you are everything.' If you are bearing a grudge against someone, deal with it! Some of you need to make phone calls, put hands out, have a coffee with someone, and say, 'I'm sorry'. Watch out if someone believes they have the ministry of authority. Watch out if someone believes they are God's gift to the church. Watch out if someone wants to dominate you. Jesus says, 'That's what the rulers of the Gentiles do, but it shall not be so among you. Whoever will be great among you, let him be your minister, let him be your servant, let him get the basin and the towel and wash your feet.'

5. Leadership must be visual

I love Peter's sermon in Acts 10. In Acts 10:38 Peter gives us an insight which is wonderful, he says, 'And [Jesus] went around doing good.' Somebody wrote, 'We're just content to just go around. He went around doing good.' Our Lord Jesus Christ practised what he preached. Remember in the Sermon on the Mount Jesus said, 'Let your light so shine before men, that they may see your good works and glorify your Father in heaven' (Matt. 5:16, NKJV). 'You are the salt of the earth . . . you are the light of the world' (Matt. 5:13,14).

Would you mind if I use a personal illustration? My mother died when I was just coming up to 14. She'd been ill since I was 7 years old. She used to smoke Woodbines, have her hair in curlers, read the Encyclopaedia Britannica to me and recite poetry. She was an absolute diamond! Some people said of my mother, 'She's the salt of the earth.' I used to think, 'What does that mean?' till I started reading my Bible.

'She's the salt of the earth!' In other words, she was all right. She was contributing to this life, she was doing good. Jesus said 'Let them see your good works and glorify your father who is in heaven.'

6. Leadership is plural

Anybody here watch the Lone Ranger? The Lone Ranger wears his cowboy hat, his black mask, and his silver guns. He jumps on his horse, rides into town and sorts all the problems out. He's called the Lone Ranger but he wasn't alone. Who was his mate? Tonto! And in churches we've got Lone Rangers but they don't have a Tonto! It's interesting in Acts 13, at a strategic point in the Acts of the Apostles, when the gospel is going to spread through Europe and the world, there's a group of spiritual men gathered to pray and fast and the Holy Spirit says, 'Separate unto me, Paul and Barnabas for the work of the ministry.' 'Now, Holy Spirit, I think you've got that a bit wrong, if you don't mind me saying. I mean Paul's enough; he knows the Old Testament inside out and back to front. Paul's enough; he's had an encounter with the risen Christ! Paul's enough.' No he isn't! It's Paul and Barnabas, then Paul and Silas, and then it will be Paul and Timothy. And when Paul establishes churches he establishes a plurality of leadership. He writes to the Philippians, to the bishops, *plural*, and deacons, *plural*, because *we* is always better than *me*. And there really is safety, accountability, encouragement and support when leadership is plural. Yes, I know it can be difficult but nevertheless remember the acronym for team:

T Together
E Each
A Achieves
M More

There is fellowship within the Godhead, God in the Trinity of his persons, and leadership in the church must be plural - teams working together for the cause of Christ.

7. Leadership must be sacrificial

Do you remember what Paul wrote to the Ephesians? He said, 'Christ loved the church and gave himself up for her' (Eph. 5:25). He gave himself, he sacrificed himself. Do you remember what Jesus said? 'The good shepherd lays down his life for the sheep' (John 10:11). If you are a leader or potential leader and you don't love the flock of God, get out! Christian leadership is wet eyes, bent knees, broken hearts, scars, and more scars.

Do you remember William Booth? He was the soldier of soup, soap and salvation. One day he's addressing an audience and with a piece of chalk draws a circle. He stands in the circle and says, 'Everything in this circle belongs to the Lord.' Then he talks to the men and women and asks 'How do you spell love?' Someone says, 'L-O-V-E'. He says 'No, you spell love S-A-C-R-I-F-I-C-E.' That's missing today, isn't it? 'If Jesus Christ be God and died for me, then no sacrifice can be too great for me to make for him' (C.T. Studd). You've got to be prepared to go the extra mile, the extra ten miles. Spiritual leadership is characterized by the cross. This is not worldly leadership, which is climbing the ladder of success to the pinnacle, crushing whoever you like in order to get there. When you get to the top of the ladder, you realize it's the wrong ladder against the wrong wall and you've wasted your time. 'For what will it profit a man if he gains the whole world, and loses his own soul?' (Mark 8:36, NKJV). We want to get to heaven and to hear from the King himself, 'Well done, good and faithful servant! . . . Come and share your master's happiness' (Matt. 25:23). And that requires going the way of the Master; a servant is not greater than his master. If Jesus was the Man of Sorrows acquainted with grief, why on earth do you think, somehow or other, that Christian leadership is a song and a dance?

8. Leadership is pastoral

When Paul is writing to the Thessalonians in 1 Thessalonians chapter 2, he says, I was like 'a mother' (v.7) and 'a father' (v.11) to you. If ever there was someone you'd think was serious and cerebral it would be the Apostle Paul. He wouldn't be the emotional sort now, would he? He wouldn't be the touchy-feely sort, would he? He wouldn't be the sort of person to put his arm around you, would he? But he's talking here as if he has pastoral, tender love: 'I was like a mother'!

We've got three lads and a girl. My daughter is a daddy's girl. She came to me once and said, 'Dad, I'm never going to get a boyfriend.' We sat on the stairs – she's crying her eyes out – I pray with her.

Two weeks later, she says, 'Dad, Dad, you're never going to believe this? So-and-so has asked me out on a date!' Great, we find out that so-and-so is tall, dark and handsome, well-off, got his own business, is a Christian and has got a car. What more do you want?!

Three weeks later he's not the One! 'He's just not the One, Dad.'

'But he's a Christian . . .'

'He's not the One, Dad.'

Sometime later . . . 'Mum, I've found him, Mike, he's great and he's a carpenter just like Jesus!'

Anyway they got married and we've got a grandson. Now I've seen a different side to my daughter. Being brought up with three lads, she's a bit of a tomboy, but you should see her with Nathan James. If anyone was made for motherhood – talk about tenderness, care, concern, and provision. Paul says that's what he was like: 'I was tender, I was loving, I was caring.' And her husband, Mike, he wants to protect his boy and teach him. Paul says, 'I was like a father – proud of my kids, protective of my kids, I wanted to teach them.' Isn't that the sort of leadership you want in your church? Leadership that is pastoral, in touch and in tune.

9. Leadership is responsible

When Paul wrote 2 Timothy 2:2 he made it plain that there is no real success in leadership without a successor. He is talking about training others. The Olympic flame will soon be carried and passed from one city to another. This is a relay race. We will be lining up and cheering on the Brits. They will be running, holding up the baton, carrying it to the next runner. Paul says we've got to pass on the baton; we've got to teach and train others; we've got to take responsibility for the equipping of leaders. There is no success without successors. Responsibility is the ability to respond, so territorialism – 'this is my little territory', 'this is my little kingdom' – should not be found in spiritual leadership. Sometimes leadership is painful, very painful, but it's the ministry of open hands - preparing others, training others, and releasing others.

10. Leadership is accountable

Paul wrote in 2 Corinthians 5:10, 'we must all appear before the judgement seat of Christ.' Do you remember Robert Murray McCheyne? Wonderfully used of God, died as a young man, he wrote this little phrase – 'Life itself is vanishing fast; prepare for eternity.' Who's the oldest man here? Who's the oldest woman? On Monday you were twenty, on Tuesday you were thirty, on Wednesday you were forty, on Thursday you were fifty, on Friday you were sixty, on Saturday you were seventy, or at least that's how quickly life seems to have gone. Agreed? Life itself is vanishing fast; we must give an account to God. Prepare for eternity, loosen your grip on this life, and strengthen your grip on eternal life! And be accountable to one another – open, nothing to hide, nothing to prove, nothing to fear. Accountable!

Leadership is vital, spiritual, credible, humble, visual, plural, sacrificial, pastoral, responsible and accountable. Who is sufficient for these things? Paul says the treasure of the gospel is put into jars of clay 'that the excellence of the power may be of God and not of us' (2 Cor. 4:7, NKJV). Listen: we are stained, charred, cracked, broken, earthen vessels. It's not about us, it's about him. May the Lord raise up spiritual leaders for our day!

God at the heart of our parenting

by Rob Parsons

Rob Parsons

Rob Parsons is an international speaker and bestselling author. In 1988 he launched Care for the Family, which has grown into a national charity with the aim to strengthen family life and help those hurting because of family difficulties. Rob has spoken live to over three-quarters of a million people in family, corporate and Christian seminars around the world. In this seminar Rob refers to his latest book, *Getting Your Kids Through Church Without Them Ending Up Hating God*.

God at the heart of our parenting

Ladies and gentlemen, before I begin, let me let you into a little secret which I'm sure is not a secret at all. When it comes to their own children, there are no experts, not the people that write the books, not the people that give the seminars or the people on television, just people trying to get their own kids through as best they can.

If we are to put the Bible at the heart of our parenting and God at the heart of our parenting this is not just a matter of us picking out some verses on parenting, this is about seeing what the Bible says about being a parent. We are fortunate in this because time and time again, when God wants to show us how he feels about us, it's the word *Father* he chooses. And when we go back to the very beginning we see God, the perfect Father, and think about this: you have God, the perfect Father, and the perfect environment and yet his children go away. One of the first things we read is God saying, 'Where are you?' How many parents of teenagers have said that? 'Where are you?' And God is saying to his children, 'Where are you? How come this has happened?'

Now the reason I wrote this book is that when our children are small we think if we do all the stuff, read all the books, it will all turn out fine, but sometimes it doesn't. I have parents coming up to me saying, 'You know my 6-year-old loves God, and my 13-year-old is in the worship band and my 16-year-old . . .' and that is wonderful. But we are looking at the long haul, college, early twenties. What can we put into our children's lives when they are small to help them get through? And just briefly I want to talk about the four main stages of a child's development in faith.

Experienced faith – this will be the child's first exposure to Christianity. For children of Christian parents it's because they have been taught about the faith, Bible stories were read to them, prayers were said with them. They are told what pleases God and what doesn't please him. They are taken to church. Experienced faith tells a child what is normal as a Christian and the fascinating thing is what the child learns here will affect their theology later in life. I meet many Christians who do not believe God actually loves them because when they were little their parents or teachers or somebody gave them the impression that God was trying to catch them out. If they prayed for half an hour it wasn't long enough. Did they read the Bible enough? Did they do this enough? And I meet people who are desperate to believe they are loved by God because in those early years nobody ever told them they were, and some have believed that the tiniest thing can make them distant from God. If you and I are going to put the Bible at the heart of our parenting and God at the heart of our parenting we have to understand these big principles. What really matters to God? What are the big things?

I remember when Lloyd was 17, he started smoking. He sat next to me in church on Sunday morning and I can smell the smoke on his clothes and I think, 'I need this like a hole in the head. I'm the chairman of Care for the Family, for goodness sake. I write books on this stuff!' And I think, 'No! Am I going to make him feel a prodigal over some smoke? No I am not.' And I can remember putting my arm on him, pulling him close and saying, 'Son, I'm so proud to have you in church with me today.' Did I want him to stop smoking? Yes. Was I glad when he did? Yes. Did I pray that he would? Yes. But am I going to make him feel an outcast for that? No. I would rather he would still be doing it but be in church next to me and have some love for God in his heart.

What are the big things that matter to God? As we try to put the Bible at the heart of our parenting, God at the heart of our parenting, we ought to say, 'Lord, what matters to you? But also help me know what doesn't matter.' And I talked about that in this book, about not sweating the small stuff. I remember a woman saying, 'A lady at my church said to me when I was 19 years old, "Godly women don't wear Doc Marten boots."' Listen, we have made millions of kids prodigals because of that kind of stuff. We have made kids feel prodigals because they had a tattoo. I'm not saying that's a good thing but we made them feel out of God's favour forever because of it, because they have a little bit of hair dye, because they did this or they did that. When we put God and the Bible at the heart of our parenting we begin with this, *God loves you.*

1 Thessalonians 5:11 says, 'encourage one another and build each other up'. If you and I are to put God at the heart of our parenting we do encourage our children, we do build them up. I'm not talking about silly flattery or necessarily building self-esteem for the sake of it – that doesn't always work – but where we can, encourage them. One of the most dynamic things I ever learnt on parenting was from Josh McDowell twenty-five years ago. He said, 'Catch your children doing something right.' You see, some of you have got a testing child, a testing teenager. Now the problem with that testing teenager is often all they hear from us is negative: 'Don't do that!' If we are really silly we compare them with their more compliant brother or sister, but we shouldn't do that because we drive wedges between the brother and sister that they might not recover from, even in later life. All they hear is negative, but is there nothing they do well? Is there nothing we can commend them for?

I remember a couple coming up to me in Canada and they said, 'Mr Parsons, we're worried about our daughter. She won't go to the youth Bible study. And she likes to go dancing on a Friday night.' She was 17 and I think, 'Well, at least she sounds normal.' But I say, 'Oh, I'm sorry.' They say, 'And she likes to go dancing on a Saturday night.' I can imagine the rows in this home. She's been out Friday night, she wants to go out Saturday night and she won't go to the youth Bible study and I say, 'Does she ever come to church with you?' And they say, 'She never misses.' I say, 'Excuse me, she never misses? You are telling me whatever time she comes in on a Saturday night she's in church with you on a Sunday morning?' 'Yes, she never misses.'

'When you go home I want you to wake her up and say that you told the preacher about your daughter and you were so proud that she's so faithful to God.' This woman looks at me and she says, 'Mr Parsons, didn't you hear what I just said to you, she won't go to youth Bible study.' I said, 'Madam, forgive me, but if you don't catch that kid doing something right you are going to have a lot more to worry about than the youth Bible study.' Catch them doing something right.

Then there is *'affiliative' faith* which is when they join in because everybody else does it. If you possibly can, get your children involved in a good youth group. And don't give the youth leader such a hard time. You know why we give youth leaders a hard time? We want them to put right in one night a week what we haven't been able to do in eighteen years. We don't read the Bible with our kids; we want the youth leader to turn these kids into theologians. We don't pray with them; we want them to pray with them all night. Pray for your youth leaders, encourage them; if you possibly can, get your kids in a strong peer group.

And then there is *searching faith* when they might begin to doubt, but that's not the end of the world. The famous doubter in the Bible is Thomas, but I think the best doubter is John the Baptist. He's been saying, 'Jesus is the Lamb of God who takes away the sin of the world,' and suddenly he's in Herod's prison and he says to his disciples, 'Go to him and say, "Are you he that should come or should we look for another?"' In other words he says, 'Have we got it wrong?' And he brings his doubts to Jesus. That's what I've encouraged my kids to do. I haven't got all the answers for them or for myself. Bring your doubts to God. He will answer many. Sometimes you have to trust till you get there.

And finally, *owned faith*. It becomes real to them. God has no grand-children. And some of you are feeling guilty because your children are not following Christ, but I'll tell you something: it's their choice ulti-mately. God has no grandchildren; every person must come into a relationship with him themselves.

Now, I want to look briefly at Deuteronomy 6:6–9. I'm sure you remember it; it talks very powerfully about traditions. In fact, when we try to put God at the heart of our parenting, the Bible at the heart of our parenting, you will find time and again in the Bible there are traditions. Traditions are very powerful in family life. Your children will forget the expensive presents you bought them, they won't forget the night you camped in the garden together and you were both so scared that at one o'clock you came indoors. They'll remember the traditions; you know what I mean, 'Dad always used to read a bit of the Bible before we slept.' 'When we were little we always said prayers together.'

I remember when my mother had Alzheimer's and had no recognition of me, it was heartbreaking. I would go to visit her and she would be lying in bed and I'd tuck the bed clothes around her as she used to for me and straighten the top sheet and then I would say, 'Shall we say prayers together?' And I would begin to whisper the words of the Lord's Prayer, my mouth next to hers, 'Our Father,' and perfectly she would begin, from that mind that could hardly string two words together. 'Our Father who art in heaven, hallowed be thy name,' and the traditions all came out. And that's why I believe that verse in Proverbs, although it is not a guarantee that everything works well, '[Bring] up a child in the way he should go, and when he is old he will not depart from it' (Prov.22:6, NKJV). There's a sense in which what you put in can never be lost. They almost can't get away from the word of God that you put in there. The Bible understood the power of traditions.

The Bible talks a lot about mealtimes. We have largely lost that in modern society but we need to eat together. Some people say you are trying to take the family back to some golden age. You know, I don't believe there ever was a golden age for the family, but I do know the power of eating a meal together. All the evidence shows it – sociologically, health-wise, educationally – eating a meal together is very powerful.

We run courses on parenting, and one day a single parent came and we were talking about the power of mealtimes and she said, 'But I don't have a table and chairs.' The person running the class said, 'Why don't you put a little blanket on the floor and sit around the blanket?' But on the way home from the class she saw a junk shop and in the window was a table and four chairs for sale. She went in and the man who owned the shop allowed her to put a £5 deposit on it, and every week when she came to the class she paid a little off, and on the last night of the class she stood up and said, 'My table and chairs are being delivered tomorrow.' What she didn't know was all the other mums had been saving and bought her a cutlery set from IKEA and a condiment set and some candles. She said, 'When we sat down the next evening we felt like kings!' The power of a simple meal together.

Just say a little, 'Thank you, Lord, for this food.' I'm not saying you have to do it but if possible, 'Lord, we thank you for this.' You know, in this book I talk about the five big killers of faith for our children, and one is familiarity. We just get too used to Jesus. We just get too used to holy things. I can remember going to a friend's house for a meal. It's a Sunday and there are eight of us around the table. He's known God, he's got a great family, God has blessed him enormously, and we are around the table and he says, 'Well, I suppose we had better say grace.' What! In a world where there's so many hungry, we sit around the table laden with food in a warm house with good friends and he says, 'I suppose we'd better say grace.' I almost felt like I heard heaven say, 'Keep it!' Familiarity is what happened to Jesus in Nazareth; they just got too used to him. 'Jesus, he mended my door.' 'We played with him in the streets.' He could have done an almighty work there, but did not because of their unbelief. Just too used to Jesus. We need to keep that sense of wonder.

Let me remind you of those verses from Deuteronomy 6:6–9:

> These commands that I give you today are to be upon your hearts. Impress them on your children. Talk about them when you sit at home and when you walk along the road, when you lie down and when you get up. Tie them as symbols on your hands and bind them on your foreheads. Write them on the door-frames of your houses and on your gates.

In other words, they are saying, make these words part of your life. When you try to put the Bible and God at the heart of your parenting it's not, as I said at the beginning, a matter of coming up with ten verses on parenting. We somehow have to live this stuff. It has to be part of our life.

You know, the problem with children is not that they don't listen to us, the problem is they do. The problem is nothing is lost, everything is formative. I've already mentioned one of the big killers of faith; let me mention another to you: cynicism. You come home on a Sunday and around the lunch table you have a little girl of 7, a boy of 9, a girl of 13 and you say, 'This church is driving me crazy. By the time we'd sung that worship song five times, I'd lost the will to live!' And your wife says 'You're the lucky one, at least you went out, we had to listen to him preach; we didn't get any decent teaching, just a bit of Beatles music and some silly stories.' Don't think you'll get away with that. You will grow cynical children and when they are 15 they'll say, 'I don't want to go there anymore; the worship's rubbish, the preaching's lame, the youth leader's tame.' Nothing is lost.

One of the next five killers of faith I talk about in the book is hypocrisy, where we give the impression to our children that we are perfect. They hear us speaking in church about the power of prayer, but they never catch us praying. They hear us speak about the need to give, but they know we never give. We talk about love, but they watch us daily, practically abusing our wife. You can get away with getting it wrong but you have to tell your children, 'Look, I'm just normal; forgive me.' They have to hear you crying; they have to see you asking others for forgiveness; they have to see you saying sorry to each other; they need to see you on your knees, 'Lord forgive me for what I've done.' That's OK, but what we can't get away with is the other stuff. The Bible says we should share our faith with others, but our kids never see us do that. We don't do anything for the neighbour – we don't even offer to mow their lawn when they are ill. They've never seen us bend to help the poor. We just don't do it. We talk about it, but we just don't do it. You can't get away from that stuff because they watch everything and they see it all.

But folks, here's the great news, you don't have to bear the guilt of being perfect; you don't have to bear the guilt of having perfect kids; we just have to be honest. The gospel is that God loves us, that when we get it wrong we come back to him. You know, Josh McDowell said, 'My little girl was 10 years old and a big TV evangelist had fallen into some scandal in America and she came running home and said,

Rob Parsons

"Daddy, Daddy, people are saying in church what terrible things that man has done." And I said, "Darling, he has done terrible things, but if he asks God's forgiveness God will forgive him. Jesus has died for him, he will forgive him." Rob, if I don't tell her that, how is she going to feel when she falls?'

Let me close with three disappointments and I talk about them in the book: three disappointments that I think are vital to get our children ready for. We've got to tell them Bible stories to get them ready for the day they will be disappointed with themselves. When Lloyd was 17 we wrote a little book together called, *What every kid wished their parents knew*. In the back of this book I've retold the story of the prodigal son because I've said this to my boy: 'No matter what you do you can always come home. You might be in a pigsty somewhere and you think you've let God down and you'll make up a little speech just like the prodigal did, but you'll never finish the speech because I'll be running for you and I'll have my arms around you. You may break my heart but you will never stop me loving you. You will never do anything that can keep you from coming home. I may be ashamed of what you've done but I will never be ashamed of you.' Tell them stories of forgiveness so that when they are disappointed with themselves they know there is a way back. This is the gospel.

Get them ready for disappointment with others. I am sorry to say this to you, but many of their deepest hurts will be at the heart of the Christian community. When we stamp and kick and fight in local churches to get our own way – 'I want the worship like this', 'I want the building like this' – and we split and we start up in the school down the road, and someone else starts up in the university down the road, we think we've got away with it. No, little kids watch as their spiritual home is blown apart. Some of their greatest hurts will be at the hands of others; some of your deepest hurts have been at the hands of other Christians. Tell them you might be hurt by them but it's not Jesus.

And finally get them ready for disappointment with God. Lily is 4 years old and she's got a goldfish called Goldie. Children aren't very adventurous with the names of their fish, as you well know. And Goldie is not very well, so they're saying prayers at night. She said,

'Mummy, I'm sorry that Goldie's not very well. Why don't we just ask Jesus to make him well?' And mother's face just sinks; she's seen the look of the goldfish when she's coming up the stairs! ' "Dear Jesus, please make my goldfish well, Amen." There it is Mummy, it's done. The Sunday School teacher told me: you ask it, you get it, done.'

The mother goes downstairs. She uses the camera on her mobile phone to take a shot of this fish which is already dead on its back in the dirty goldfish bowl. She rushes out to Pet World. The manager of Pet World has seen this thing a hundred times. It takes him about ten minutes to find a fish pretty much like Goldie and mum goes home and puts it in the bowl. The little girl runs downstairs the next day, 'Mummy, Mummy, Jesus has answered our prayers. He's even made him fatter.'

Did that Mum do well? Perhaps she did, but she can't go on like that because that kid will pray for her best friend to be healed of cancer and her best friend will seem to be healed for six months but then she'll cry by a graveside. I meet men and women in their mid-life turning their back on God the second life goes wrong for them. A man 45 years of age, he's lived a charmed life. He's had a wonderful ministry, lovely home, lovely wife, kids and at 45 he loses his job. And on the day he loses his job he loses his faith. Get your kids ready for that day when it seems that God hasn't given them all they want. Tell them it even happened with the Lord Jesus. 'Father if it is possible let this cup pass from me,' and God says, 'No,' even to his own Son.

And pray for your children, if you are married and you have children and you are not praying together for your kids, start tonight. Put up your hands if you have toddlers? Do you ever look forward to the day when they will be grown and you won't have to worry about them? Watch this! I can frighten the life out of you. Anybody here with kids in their thirties or forties? Do you still worry about them? More than ever, that's why you must pace yourselves. You know sometimes the older they get the harder it is; you love so much but we don't have control. Pray for your children. Don't carry the guilt of them not being perfect, but pray for them.

As I went around the world with the *Bringing Home the Prodigal* message, I would often go into a city two months before the main event and get all the church leaders together. And I'm in a city and a young man comes up to me and says, 'Rob, I'm a youth pastor and this is the first day on the job.' I shake his hand and say, 'Congratulations.' He says, 'My mother wanted me to say hello to you.' I say, 'Oh, do I know your mother?' He says, 'No, but in the Birmingham National Exhibition Centre three years ago (when we had four thousand people praying for their prodigals) she brought my name and put it at the foot of the cross for prayer, and you didn't know it, but as you were praying my name was there.'

So when I go to the city for the main event I tell that story and, as I'm walking down the aisle, somebody pulls my coat and I turn and this woman looks up at me and she says, 'I'm the mother. I am that mother.' And as I look into her eyes it's as if she's saying, 'I am the mother who waited for his key in the door in the early hours of the morning. I am the mother who cried. I am the mother who almost gave up. I am the mother who prayed.' Thank God for the mothers who pray. Don't ever give up; don't lose heart; God loves your kids a million times more than even you do and he loves you too. May God give us wisdom as we seek to put him and his Word at the heart of our parenting.

The Word @ 2.30

The disciple and mission

by Ken Clarke

Ken Clarke

Ken Clarke grew up in Holywood, Co. Down. He is married to Helen and they have four daughters and five grandchildren. He has served in parishes in Northern Ireland, in Chile with SAMS, and Crinken, Dublin. Before moving to his present role as Bishop of Kilmore, Elphin and Ardagh in January 2001, he was Rector of Coleraine Parish for 15 years. He has led missions and preached at conferences and conventions in different parts of the world.

The disciple and mission: Isaiah 50:4–11

Like so much of Scripture this passage is a gold mine and the more we dig the more gold we find. In this passage there is such a revelation of who God is. Four times in verses 4–9 we read the phrase, 'Sovereign LORD', and he is the Sovereign Lord. Isn't it amazing how often things we say with our lips are not really matched with faith in our hearts? How many church meetings have we been at which have quite rightly opened in prayer and we've prayed to God, the Creator God, the Redeemer, the Sovereign Lord and so on. And then the first item on the agenda is discussed and everybody's in depression, 'What are we going to do? There's no way through this.' And yet a few minutes before we have been praying to the Sovereign Lord!

The Sovereign Lord is the maker of heaven and earth, the teacher, the provider, the helper, the giver. John Piper compares biblical revelation as just the tip of an iceberg. Most of God's majesty is out of sight, and even what is revealed in the Bible is so massive that it extends beyond our ability to comprehend it.

I have to say that Isaiah 50 is a classic example of this; we are catching a glimpse of the tip of the iceberg. But, dear friends, if we only catch a glimpse of who the Sovereign Lord is, we will be astounded, we will be astonished, we will be humbled, we will be overwhelmed, for he is in control; he is supreme; he is God; there is no other. And in this servant song the Sovereign Lord prepares the servant for ministry, he stands by the servant in adversity and he helps the servant in difficulty. As we read it we discover our Sovereign God is the giver, the teacher, and the helper.

First of all, the Sovereign Lord is the giver. Look at how it starts: 'the Sovereign LORD has given me an instructed tongue'. Or as another translation puts it, 'the Sovereign LORD has given me a well-instructed tongue.' Isn't this exactly what the Lord gave to Isaiah and the other prophets, an instructed tongue, a well-taught tongue? They didn't just teach and preach, they actually were well-taught. And in this passage the servant comes to us as a disciple, for a disciple is one who is taught. He was not endowed with an instant gift but over a period of time he has been taught, he has been absorbing what the Sovereign Lord has been saying; he was trained. Behind his instructed tongue is training, training, training and isn't that a mark of a disciple?

In Northern Ireland – I presume it's the same in England – when someone is learning to drive they put a white square on their front window and rear window with a red 'L' on it signifying that they are learners. A disciple is a learner, and in this passage we discover the servant is learning from the Sovereign Lord who has instructed him. I think it's important to remember that it is God who gives the gift, the call, the instruction. In God's family we do not invent, create or manufacture ministry. No, it's a calling and it's God who calls us. No Christian pastor, preacher, or leader is self-appointed; it's a response to a call of the Sovereign Lord. Read Isaiah 6.

I just wonder if in some parts of the church we have lost sight of – the old word used to be – vocation? We think if we do a particular course, a particular programme or read a particular book we'll get whatever's being talked about. But it doesn't work that way; it's God who calls. It could be a young shepherd boy, it could be a farmer, it could be a businessman, it could be a student. It is God who calls and on that call his ministry is built. Do you remember when Jesus stood up in the synagogue in his home town Nazareth? He was handed the book of the prophet Isaiah and read, 'The Spirit of the LORD is upon me for he has anointed me.' It's his call, it's his anointing and we are privileged to hear his call and be under his anointing. We must never, ever forget that.

Do you remember when Paul was writing to a group of discouraged Christians in Corinth, losing heart, thinking of giving up, and he says, 'Since we have received this ministry we do not lose heart.' This ministry is a call, a gift, it's a treasure we've received. Like his Lord before him, Paul recognized that all we have and all that we are is a gift, not reward. I worry when people function on a theology of reward – 'If I live a good life I'll get brownie points.' It's not like that, is it? It's not about, 'if I, if I, if I, if I.' It's about him, him, him, him. It's about what he does, what he has done, what he will do. He is the giver and the author of salvation. He is the giver of gifts; he is the one who calls us to ministry, and here in Isaiah he has given his servant an instructed tongue. The teacher is not self-appointed, but has been called by God, and we are told here he has been well-taught. He has an instructed tongue; he has absorbed God's teaching.

Why was he given an instructed tongue? Verse 4: 'The Sovereign Lord has given me an instructed tongue, to know the word that sustains the weary.' I wonder, when we have grown weary how often we have turned to the book of the prophet Isaiah? How often have we read and been refreshed and inspired with these words from Isaiah 40:28–31?

> Do you not know? Have you not heard? The Lord is the everlasting God, the Creator of the ends of the earth. He will not grow tired or weary, and his understanding no one can fathom. He gives strength to the weary and increases the power of the weak. Even youths grow tired and weary, and young men stumble and fall; but those who hope in the Lord will renew their strength. They will soar on wings like eagles; they will run and not grow weary, they will walk and not be faint.

Praise God for those words, they are true. This is the word of truth. And as you and I know in our walk with God again and again we've grown weary and the Lord has refreshed us, we keep going, we start soaring like the eagles. His words have brought hope and refreshment to the weary, the tired, the burnt-out, the worn out.

I don't know what it's like this side of the Irish Sea, but in Ireland I can tell you many Christians are exhausted, tired out, emotionally drained. I remember listening to a church leader for whom I had huge respect. He told me one day he went into his church office and a secretary said to him, 'Rector, are you not taking the funeral today?' He said 'What funeral?' Never in his whole ministry had that wonderful man of God ever forgotten a funeral. Within one hour he was in hospital totally exhausted, physically, emotionally. You see, what many people in the church didn't know was that for the previous three nights he had been up every night dealing with emergencies and working a full day, and this was a build-up after months and months of busyness. The guy was just exhausted.

I think of somebody who had a huge influence in my wife's life when she was a young Christian. He poured himself into young people, he was someone whom God wonderfully used but he burnt out. And for years he just limped along as a Christian; he even gave up going to church for a while. He and I started meeting for the occasional cup of coffee or lunch together and I'll never forget something he said to me. He said, 'You know, Ken, in my work (he worked in a docks area; he was in a very senior position in the firm) from Monday to Friday I have to tell you I get battered every day of the week. I can't cope with the church where I get battered on a Sunday.' And, dear friends, sometimes the church needs to recapture this vision here of a word for the weary because sometimes we can wound the wounded and we can edge the weary towards depression because of a lack of compassion and understanding and a word that refreshes, encourages, refills and refuels. This is what our Jesus does, the Sovereign King, the Servant King.

Our churches should be green pastures and still waters for the Lord's sheep. Some preachers seem to think Jesus said, 'Fleece the sheep.' He didn't; he said, 'Feed the sheep.' I'm not a farmer and I'm sure there are some of you here who know far more about sheep than I do, but in Ireland the sheep are shorn once a year but they are fed every day. Sometimes in the church we reverse that and the sheep are shorn every week and if they get fed once a year, well, that's an added bonus. Jesus is the good shepherd, he cares for the weary sheep, the tired, the exhausted, the burnt out. And I guess some of us have arrived this week at Keswick and quite frankly we're exhausted. And one of the things we need this week is to meet Jesus again, the one who whispers into our hearts, 'Come to me all who are weak and heavy laden and I will give you rest.' Are we listening?

I love Eugene Peterson's paraphrase of those words of Jesus in Matthew 11:28–30 (*The Message*):

> Are you tired? Worn out? Burned out on religion? Come to me. Get away with me and you'll recover your life. I'll show you how to take a real rest. Walk with me and work with me – watch how I do it. Learn the unforced rhythms of grace. I won't lay anything heavy or ill-fitting on you. Keep company with me and you'll learn to live freely and lightly.

I wonder, are those God's words for some of us here? What we need above all else this week is a word from God that will sustain us and refresh us because, quite frankly, we are weary.

Secondly, the Sovereign Lord is the teacher. The second half of verse 4 says, 'He wakens me morning by morning, wakens my ear to listen like one being taught.' One commentator has written of these words, 'The servant is a disciple before he is anything else and as such his outstanding characteristic is attentiveness to God.' Attentiveness to God – morning by morning God instructs him and morning by morning he listens. Alec Motyer says that ears eager to receive the word of God are the primary mark of a disciple. I wonder how are your ears? Are they in listening mode during this week at Keswick? The Sovereign Lord 'wakens me morning by morning, wakens my ear to listen like one being taught.' Wasn't this a mark of Jesus? What did he often do early in the morning? Mark 1:35: 'Very early in the morning, while it was still dark, Jesus got up, left the house and went off to a solitary place, where he prayed.' And remember, prayer isn't just talking, it is also listening. I wonder, do we ever get up early just to listen, to spend time with the Lord?

An old friend of mine and a man who had a wonderful influence on generations of Christian leaders in Northern Ireland was a bank manager called T.S. Mooney. He was a great man for particular sayings and one of them was, 'There are Christians who spend their time going from one convention to another looking for a blessing and the best blessing you could give them is a good alarm clock.' Now, he did have a point. I wonder, do we make time to listen to the Lord? Whether it is early in the morning, whether it is mid-morning, in the afternoon or late at night – whenever it is, are we developing this attentiveness to our God? He wants to speak into each of our lives through his Word. The verse says, 'He wakens my ear to listen.' Honestly, how good are we at listening? The servant of the Lord is a listener. There are so many voices in our culture today, whose voice do we listen to? Don't we see so many people, young, middle-aged and indeed elderly, listening to the wrong voices and therefore going the wrong way? What did Jesus say? 'Man does not live on bread alone, but on every word that comes from the mouth of God' (Matt. 4:4). Are we building into our lives attentiveness to the Lord? It is high-octane priority. And, incidentally, the word that is used for listening here in verse 4 carries the sense of lifelong attentive listening. And I wonder, do some of us need to rediscover that openness to the Lord, that attentiveness to God's voice?

And then, the Sovereign Lord is our helper. Look at verse 7: 'Because the Sovereign LORD helps me, I will not be disgraced.' And verse 9: 'It is the Sovereign LORD who helps me. Who is he who will condemn me? They will all wear out like a garment; the moths will eat them up.' In verse 7, the servant knows the Lord's help in the midst of opposition and suffering. And in verse 9 he knows the Lord's help in the midst of accusations, of criticisms, of condemnation. Whatever the believer faces, and sometimes it is not very pleasant, God is our helper. And I wonder, is that the truth that some of us need to take away to meditate on after looking at this passage? The Sovereign Lord helps us and he wants to.

I'm sure these words have come into your mind this week in this beautiful setting of Keswick: 'I lift up my eyes to the hills – where does my help come from? My help comes from the LORD, the Maker of heaven and earth' (Ps. 121:1–2). You know, I used to think I knew what the Psalmist meant by those words. You look at the hills and the mountains – aren't they beautiful, aren't they stunning? It was the Lord, the maker of heaven and earth, who made them and wants to help us. But one Bible commentator I was reading gave a very interesting insight to those words. He said, 'The context of this is very often, in the time of the psalmist, fertility rites, occult practices, and the worship of false gods would take place in the hills.' So what the Psalmist is really saying is, 'I will lift up my eyes to the hills. Up in the hills are all those people seeking help from false gods. Where does my help come from? It comes from the LORD, the maker of the heavens and earth.' Isn't that a wonderful insight? God and God alone is our helper. Isn't it amazing along how many avenues people are looking for help today? The stars, horoscopes, fortune tellers, tarot cards, crystals, stones, on and on we could go. Our help comes from the Lord. The help we really need is from the Sovereign Lord.

Now, what do all these truths here mean – what are they saying to us about the servant King Jesus? Verse 4: he is one who receives, and as we read the gospels we see that again and again what Jesus has received from the Father, he is passing onto us. Secondly, Jesus is one who was well-taught – even at 12 years old he was teaching in the temple, was he not? Thirdly, we see in his life and ministry his teaching bringing a word of refreshment. Fourthly, Jesus is one who listens. He listened to his father and he listened to people. Fifthly, he was one who obeyed. A life of utter obedience was one of the supreme marks of Jesus. Look at verse 5 again, 'The Sovereign LORD has opened my ears, and I have not been rebellious; I have not drawn back.' Sixthly, verse 6 and onwards, Jesus was one who suffered. Did not Jesus suffer misunderstanding, denial, betrayal? One of the toughest things any of us can face is betrayal from one of our best friends and, folks, it happens. It happened to Jesus. Think of Gethsemane, the time he needed those disciples, those closest to him, the time he needed them the most – what were they doing? Sleeping. Jesus knew all about suffering and I haven't even mentioned the cross. Seventhly, he was one who persevered. Look at verse 7: 'Because the Sovereign LORD helps me, I will not be disgraced. Therefore have I set my face like flint, and I know I will not be put to shame.' The gospels tell us that Jesus set his face to go to Jerusalem; he wouldn't turn back or opt out. He knew what was facing him there but he went for you and for me. And finally, verses 8 and 10, he was one who utterly trusted and relied on

Ken Clarke

his Father. What were some of those words of Jesus on the cross? 'Father into your hands I commit my spirit.' In the garden – 'Father, not my will but yours be done.' He trusted and relied on his Father.

Now finally, how does all this relate to the sons and daughters of God, the servants of the King of Kings? Well, we are called to be like him, aren't we? We are to be receptive, teachable, listening, persevering, open, obedient, trusting – do we see these marks in the lives of Christ's followers today? Are these marks of our churches today? Has obedience a high-octane priority? Is perseverance a mark of our lives? Do we just give up easily? There is a cost to obedience and sometimes we don't want that cost, yet Jesus says we are to take up our cross and follow him. And there is a big question here we need to answer in the final part of this passage. Look at verse 10: 'Who among you fears the LORD and obeys the word of his servant? Let him who walks in the dark, who has no light, trust in the name of the LORD and rely on his God.' You see, there is a choice here: obedience in verse 10 or disobedience described in verse 11: 'But now, all you who light fires and provide yourselves with flaming torches, go, walk in the light of your fires and of the torches you have set ablaze.' To a society and a culture that is all about self we need to hear these words. And what if we choose to go the self way – what is the outcome of that? Well, that's the latter part of verse 11, 'This is what you shall receive from my hand: You will lie down in torment.' That way is literally a dead end, a place of torment, a Godless cul-de-sac. The path of obedience is the way the servant King went and it is the way we are called to go. The choice is ours: disobedience, or the way of the true disciple, the faithful servant. The path of obedience was costly for Isaiah, for Jesus the Servant King, and it will be for us.

I want to finish on a personal note. When I was invited to speak on this passage I couldn't quite believe it. And I will tell you why. Some years ago I had been invited to preach in the North West of Uganda, the diocese of Nebbi. The bishop there at that time was Bishop Henry Orombi who is now the Archbishop of Uganda. And we went thinking that the diocese's convention that I was invited to preach at would be two or three hundred people; it was actually three or four thousand people. Some had walked two days to get there. It was a time we will never forget. And when we were there, Henry told us the diocese had just bought a mountain – as you do. Why had they bought a mountain? Because they had heard about prayer mountains in Korea where Christians, individuals, small groups would go and they would pray, and they would pray, and they would pray. Many people say one of the secrets of the growth of the church in South Korea is their commitment to prayer. And Henry wanted to take me to this prayer mountain. It was quite a distance. We eventually got to this mountain which to me seemed to be in the middle of nowhere. And I will never forget – we got out of the car and we chatted for a few minutes and he explained that this was all forest. And he said, 'Right, this is Prayer Mountain and we are going to pray. I am going to go away and pray for a few hours and you can pick a spot too. You pray and I will come back.' And I thought 'Yes, Henry!'

When you are a little bit fearful, do you ever have totally irrational thoughts? Here I was on this remote mountain, in the middle of nowhere, looking over to the Congo. He disappeared and I was on my own and I thought, 'Oh, no – wild animals, poisonous snakes, Congolese rebels from the neighbouring country.' I had the whole lot happening to me in the next couple of hours! But then I thought, 'Just hold on.' All I had with me was my Bible, and I am ashamed to tell you that I couldn't remember the last time I had been out in a lonely place with just my Bible and the Lord. We can learn a lot from our African brothers. And I had one of the most special times of my whole life with the Lord during those few hours. I came away from that mountain and imprinted in my heart, mind and soul were these words, 'The Sovereign LORD has given me an instructed tongue, to know the word that sustains the weary. He wakens me morning by morning, wakens my ear to listen like one being taught' – it is highlighted. I said, 'Thank you, God. I believe that is part of your call on my life'. And ten and a half years after becoming a bishop I wanted a simple bishop's ring which just has a cross on it and inside there are two texts and one of them is Isaiah 50:4.

Can I just say this: the text from Isaiah 50 may be inscribed in this little ring but, brothers and sisters, it is far more important that these truths are written deeply in all of our hearts and lives. The way of the

servant is listening to his Master's voice and obeying his Word, whatever the cost. God bless you as you walk that path of obedience, and
let us encourage one another with words that will refresh and sustain
the weary.

The Addresses

Why Mission?

by John Risbridger

John Risbridger

John Risbridger is a Trustee of Keswick Ministries and works at Above Bar Church in Southampton as Minister and Team Leader. After five years in hospital management, he spent ten years working with UCCF – first as a regional team leader and then as Head of Student Ministries. At the heart of his ministry is the desire to see a passion for the glory of God and the supremacy of Christ energizing our theology, our worship and our mission, all at the same time. He is married to Alison and they have two teenage daughters.

Why mission? Genesis 12:1–9

Well, it is great to be back at Keswick. I missed last year but two years ago I was here and you know what, it was raining in Keswick – can you believe it? I was down by the lake camping with my family and it rained so much that by the middle of the week you couldn't tell the difference between the campsite and Derwentwater. One morning I woke up and looked outside the tent and I saw a family of swans swimming by. I am not exaggerating - it really happened!

But it is great to be back. And what a theme we have before us for the Convention this year – *Word to the World*. As you have already heard, it is four hundred years since the King James Version of the Bible was published. Have you ever asked yourself what it would have been like to hold in your hands one of those first copies? I wonder what that would have felt like. The sense of joy, the sense of history, the sense of standing at the beginning of a great story in which the Word of God had been let loose among the people, spoken in the language of the people, so it can transform and shape a nation and a culture as it has done. It would have been extraordinary to have been there, wouldn't it?

I had an experience not so long ago that was a little bit like that particular moment in history. Just three days ago I led a funeral of one of our church mission partners. She had battled with cancer for thirteen years. Her name was Gillian. Gillian, with her husband Keir, gave over thirty years of their lives to translate the Bible into the language of a group of about a hundred thousand people that live in central and northern Ghana. She and her husband completed the job just two years before her death. That means for eleven years she battled on with the task while battling on with cancer.

Well, last November I had the opportunity to go to Ghana with them to share in the service of dedication in which we gave the Scriptures to the Chumburung people. Can you imagine what that was like? For the first time in their history they had the Word of God in their own language. They held it in their hands. It was an unforgettable moment. A little bit like the moment the King James Version was first published in Britain, I suspect. This was, if you like, their moment. When the Word of God was given to them as a people and it was welcomed with enormous joy. I can't think of a better illustration of what this year's Convention is all about – Word for the World. And wouldn't it be wonderful if during this week God called a number of us to give our lives, as Gillian gave her life, to bring the Scriptures to another people group who don't yet have them in their own language?

But I want to begin this week by painting a very broad picture of mission, a picture in which people like Gillian play a key part, but also a picture in which every one of us as Christians have a part to play. Why mission? That is the question. The answer must be fundamentally because God is himself a God of mission. God has a mission, a glorious mission which he is pursuing in the world, and to be the people of God is to share in his mission. And that means all of us, whoever we are and wherever we are. If we belong to the people of God, we are called to be partners in his mission in the world.

What is that mission? What is it that God is doing in the world? Let me tell you another story. In 1986, there was a small delegation of Christian leaders who travelled to Moscow in order to make representations to the Minister for Religious Affairs. They were speaking up for persecuted and imprisoned Christians within the Soviet Union. Remember, this is 1986, this is a Russia that is still shaped by Khrushchev's claim that he would parade the last Christian in Russia on state television and then that would be the end of the church of Jesus Christ. The delegation was met with a hostile reception from the

Minister. The Minister asked how they could dare lecture him in the light of the gross failures of the West and in particular of the evangelical church in the West. That was 1986.

In 2010, a member of the same delegation returned to Moscow. He went to visit a large conference of Baptists and evangelical Christians and it was large. How wrong Khrushchev had been. He must still be turning in his grave at the shock. Their message had clearly been spreading and bearing fruit. But the really striking thing was this: the meeting was attended by a representative from the president's office and also from the office of the mayor of Moscow. And that representative began her speech on behalf of the mayor of Moscow by looking at this vast conference of Christians and thanking them for all that they were contributing to their society. Can you believe that? Thanking them for feeding the hungry, for welcoming the refugees and for caring for people when everybody else had given up and gone home.

I think it is a nice story. It's a true story because I know the guy who went. It was David Coffey, a former trustee of Keswick. But what do you make of that story? Is this evidence that actually the Russian churches are having a bit of an identity crisis? And frankly need to get back to being a church rather than doing the work of social services for them? Or is it evidence that in sharing the message in words of truth and actions of practical love those churches have understood, perhaps better than many of us, what it really means to be the people of God in the world and to share in his mission?

I suppose the answer to the question will depend on what you think God's mission actually is. So let's get back to Genesis to discover the first answer to the question: why mission, and what is God doing in the world? Why mission? Well, firstly because God has promised to bless the nations, that is our passage this evening, Genesis 12. Let's put it in context. The Bible, of course, begins with this wonderful vision of how God wants the world to be, and what God created human beings to be. I think that vision remains the most compelling vision for human life the world has ever had. And we need to recover our confidence in that vision and express it more clearly. It is a vision of human beings in a right and joyful relationship with God, bearing his image within creation, sharing something of his creativity and joy and as his image bearers, possessing inestimable dignity and awesome responsibility to care for creation on God's behalf. What a vision of human life that is.

Genesis 1:28 describes it in these terms, 'God blessed them'. Note that language: 'God blessed them and said to them, "Be fruitful and increase in number; fill the earth and subdue it."' But how did the human story continue? Well, rather than live within this blessing of God, the tragedy of our race is that we chose to try and create our own vision of human life, rather than embrace the one that God had given us. And the vision of human life that we created for ourselves was one in which God was pushed to the margins, if he was there at all. We wanted to be our own gods. Genesis 3–11 describes that tragic choice and all of its consequences – in social breakdown, in ecological crisis and stress, in human arrogance and, of course, in death itself. You see, what has happened, the blessing of the God–centred life for which we were created, has been replaced with a curse: the curse of alienation from God.

But then in Genesis 12 something begins to change as God speaks to Abraham. God says, 'I will make you into a great nation and I will bless you' (v.2). You see that language recurring again: 'I will bless you'. Instead of the curse, we've got a promise, a blessing. But why will God bless Abraham? God will bless Abraham in order that he should be a blessing. 'I will make you into a great nation and I will bless you; I will make your name great, and you will be a blessing' (v.2). Now, just stop there for a moment because that is huge. I wonder if you have come to Keswick this week hoping that God will bless you. I hope you have and I hope he does. I'm sure he will. But why? Why does God bless us? Why is God going to bless you and me this week at Keswick? For what purpose?

Is it to just to give us another bless-up? So we go home happy and buoyed up? Now let's be very clear, God blesses us as his people in order to make us a blessing in the world. He blesses us so that we are equipped to share in his great mission. You see the chain of blessing that goes on. God blesses us in order that we may bless others and call them to faith so that they may experience the blessing and then go on to bless others. And, brothers and sisters, what I want to say to you this week is, don't let the chain of blessing stop with you, because that is not the purpose of God. That is not why he has brought you to Keswick. God blesses in order that we may be a blessing as his people in the world, and then just see the scope of his purposes. They are global, aren't they? See verse 3: 'I will bless those who bless you, and whoever curses you I will curse; and all peoples on earth will be blessed through you.' All of the nations impacted by the blessing of God through his people. Here, I believe, is the essential mission of God. He has set out to bless the nations through blessing Abraham and his offspring. Just as the curse of Genesis 3 brought damage and alienation to every aspect of human life, so this promised blessing will bring healing and restoration to every aspect of human life.

Let me just bring out three practical implications for you:

1. God's mission spans the whole of the Bible, not just the New Testament. Do you know, God did not just think up the idea of world mission when he wrote Mathew 28. No, it was in his heart right from the beginning. Sometimes we think that in the Old Testament God was just interested in Israel and in the New Testament he became a bit more broad-minded and started to love the world. No, right here at the beginning of the Old Testament it couldn't be clearer: the mission of God is to bring his blessing to all the nations of the world. The mission spans all of the Bible.

2. God's mission embraces all nations not just Israel. Of course, it was one of the great temptations of Israel as the people of God to try and keep the blessing to themselves as if the promise to Abraham stopped at the beginning of verse 2. And aren't we the same? So often we think, 'Well, if God will deliver for me then I am happy enough with that, as long as I get my blessing.' But that is not the point of the mission of God. He blessed Abraham and his offspring so that through them all the nations would be blessed and he blesses us, so that through us, all the nations may be blessed.

3. God's mission impacts the whole of creation, not just what we call the *spiritual side of life*, although it is pretty hard to figure out what

we mean by the *spiritual side of life* since Jesus is Lord of the whole of creation. It is tempting, isn't it, for us to read a rather narrow thinking into this language of blessing, but I want to suggest that when we do that we are misreading Genesis. Let's be clear: by its very nature, blessing comes from God. And therefore the ultimate blessing has got to be, to know him through his Son, Jesus Christ. But let's also be clear that in the Bible the blessed life is not only a life of personal piety and holiness. No, the blessed life is a life of restored and authentic humanness so that we begin to fulfil our role in creation of bringing fruitfulness and order and blessing once again. As we saw in Genesis 1:28, the outworking of the blessing of God is not just in what we call the *spiritual sphere*, it's in the sphere of creation as well, as human beings fill the earth and harness its resources. In other words, God's blessing is about things being put right, restoring people to God who made them for himself, restoring people as people and so restoring them to fulfilling their role in creation so that they then act as agents of restoration, of justice and of blessing in creation. Are you seeing the scope of the mission of God? It impacts the whole of creation.

Do you want an example? Just think of Genesis 39 and the story of Joseph. Genesis 39:2: 'The LORD was with Joseph and he prospered' – Joseph is blessed. And it continues, 'The LORD blessed the household of the Egyptian because of Joseph' – Joseph became a blessing (v.5). And what Joseph did for Potiphar's household he went on to do for the whole of Egypt. Isn't that wonderful? You see, Joseph wasn't a preacher. He wasn't what we would call a missionary. No, he was a slave and then later on a rather eminent civil servant. But in those, apparently secular roles, he was fulfilling the mission of God as he brought the blessing of God to the nations. Doesn't that change the way you think about Monday morning? Doesn't it change the way you think about your work, about your engagement in the community, about everyday life in its ordinariness? Doesn't it change the way you think about mission and your part in it? Mission isn't just for the missionaries, though we are right to honour them and we love the work that they do. Mission is for all of God's people.

So here then is God's vast agenda, his mission in the world. He blesses us, so that we may become a blessing, and that blessing has these vast restorative dimensions in all the nations of the world. But here's the question: how does this promise to Abraham get fulfilled as the narrative of Scripture unfolds? Well, just come with me to the New Testament. Galatians 3:14: 'He redeemed us in order that the blessing given to Abraham' – we know what that is now – 'might come to the Gentiles through Christ Jesus, so that by faith we might receive the promise of the Spirit.' Isn't that stunning? The promise made to Abraham is ultimately fulfilled in and through Jesus Christ. So, why mission? Number one, because God has a plan to bless the nations.

Why mission? Number two, because God sent his Son to bless the nations. Jesus fulfils the promise. How does he fulfil the promise? How did he lift the curse of God and replace it with the blessing of God? Well, the answer is here in Galatians 3:13: 'Christ redeemed us from the curse of the law by becoming a curse for us, for it is written: "Cursed is everyone who is hung on a tree."' Jesus fulfilled the promise to Abraham by going to the cross where he took the curse on himself so that it could be lifted from us. And having lifted the curse from us he was able to bring God's blessing to us, as we have seen in verse 14. In the New Testament just as in the Old, the scope of the blessing is, again, vast. Hear these words from Colossians 1:19–20: 'God was pleased to have all his fullness dwell in him, and through him to reconcile to himself all things, whether things on earth or things in heaven, by making peace through his blood, shed on the cross.' Why mission? Because God sent his Son to bless the nations.

And then back in Galatians 3, one final theme. Why mission? Well, have a look at verses 6–9: 'Consider Abraham: "He believed God, and it was credited to him as righteousness." Understand, then, that those who believe are children of Abraham.' Verse 8 is the key verse: 'The Scripture foresaw that God would justify the Gentiles by faith, and announced the gospel in advance to Abraham: "All nations will be blessed through you." So those who have faith are blessed along with Abraham, the man of faith.' Those who have faith are children of Abraham. What was the promise at the beginning? That it would be through the offspring of Abraham that the promise of blessing the nations would be fulfilled. Who are the offspring of Abraham? Well, of course, the supreme answer to that question is, Jesus, the true seed of Abraham.

But by faith, we, the people of God, are joined to him, and we therefore are also the children of Abraham. God's plan is to bless the nations through the offspring of Abraham, and therefore his plan is to bless the nations through you and me who own the name of Jesus Christ, for we are Abraham's children. God has a great mission in the world. This agenda of blessing runs all through the Bible – it encompasses all of the nations, includes all of God's people, will bring restoration to all of creation through the cross and, would you believe it, he has put you and me at the heart of his plan.

We love the work of those who serve as full-time partners in mission across the world, and we should honour them because we live in a society that doesn't know how to honour Christian missionaries, and therefore the church of Jesus should. But is mission only for them? Did God say that he would fulfil his mission of blessing the nations only through a select few? No, it was through all the believing children of Abraham – Jew and Gentile – that the promise would be fulfilled. God is a God of mission. A God with a mission, and therefore to be the people of God we must be partners with him in that mission. That is why God has brought you to Keswick this year. He does want to bless you this week because he is like that. He is a God of enormous generosity and lavish grace, a God of rich mercy, who loves to bring his blessing into the lives of the people he loves and cherishes – that is you and me. He loves to bless us. He wants to bless us this week, but it cannot stop there. He blesses us that we might be a blessing in the nations.

Let me give you three challenges to take away at the start of this week. Number one, will you be a blessing in your everyday life? You see, we are so locked into the idea that mission is about going that we have lost the sense that some of mission is simply about being the people of God wherever we are, and then, like Joseph, bringing his blessing there. You see, before we were called to anything else as human beings we were called to bring fruitfulness and order and blessing in creation. And, friend, when you do that in your workplace, in your community, in your home and in your family, when you treat people well, when you use energy and resources responsibly, when you care for the vulnerable you are involved in the mission of God. Make no mistake about it. And as we act to bless our communities our testimony to Christ is made attractive and credible. Will you be a blessing in your everyday life?

Number two: will you be a blessing through your church community? I wonder if you know Krish Kandiah? He came and did a day at our church a little while ago and asked us this very searching question: if your church had to close down who would notice that it had gone? What about your church? If it had to close down who would notice that it had gone? Would it, frankly, only be the Christians? Or would the hungry in your town and city notice? Would the broken notice? Would the mums who are struggling as single parents notice? Would the confused and searching who are looking for credible answers notice? Who would notice if your church shut down? We are called to be a people of blessing reaching out with words of truth and with actions of love. Is your church a blessing in your community?

Number three: will you be a part of blessing the nations? Because blessing the nations in the name of Christ is a massive privilege. It lies at the very heart of the mission of God, and this week I'm sure we will learn much more about what that can involve for us. It's about blessing them with the Bible in their own language. It's about blessing them with the good news of Jesus Christ so that they can be reconciled to God. It's about blessing the hungry with food and the poor with help. It is about blessing the oppressed with justice and hope for the needy. Will you be involved in blessing the nations? Will you use your talents, your time and your treasure for the glory of Christ, to advance the mission and purpose of God in the world?

Why mission? Because God is a God of mission. Why mission? Because God has promised to bless the nations. Why mission? Because God has sent his Son to bless the nations. Why mission? Because God calls his people to bless the nations. What a tragedy it would be if that chain of blessing stopped with you or with me. Let's just go back to those churches in Moscow being thanked by their mayor for their contribution to their city. Don't you think that the people in Moscow might be more open to their message as they see it lived out in practical love and compassion? Don't you think that it honours Jesus Christ when his people are making such a valuable contribution to the welfare of their city? Don't you think that it is rather like Jesus himself to love people, both with actions of love and with words of truth? Don't you think perhaps that those Russian Christians have learnt some of the scope of what it means to bless their city in the name of Christ? That is the mission of God and it must therefore be the mission of his people. But my question for you is: are you willing to make his mission your mission too?

For what purpose?

by Patrick Fung

Patrick Fung

Patrick Fung is currently the General Director of OMF International (formerly the China Inland Mission). He and his wife, Dr Jennie Fung, previously served as medical missionaries in South Asia for a number of years. Patrick is actively involved in missionary training and preaching ministry, being one of the plenary speakers at Urbana 2009 and the Third Lausanne Congress for World Evangelization in 2010. Patrick has two children: Elaine aged 18, and Samuel aged 12.

For what purpose? Psalm 97

God is sovereign. And this is not irrelevant to us as I checked out the dates today on the Internet. More than a year ago there was the volcano eruption from Iceland where half of the sky in Europe was paralysed, the air traffic was paralysed and people could not get home. Everything ground to a halt. And yet today we know that we are people with hope, we live confidently. Here we read Psalm 97. Psalm 97 belongs to a group of psalms, Psalms 93–99, that declare, 'The LORD reigns!' Psalms 93, 97 and 99, all begin with this phrase, 'The LORD reigns.' This phrase, 'The LORD reigns,' cannot, should not, be declared in a very sterile, monotonous, flat way. It should be declared with strong convictions, emotions and with excitement. I can quote from the book of Isaiah 52:7: 'How beautiful on the mountains are the feet of those who bring good news, who proclaim peace, who bring good tidings, who proclaim salvation, who say to Zion, "Your God reigns!"'

This is good news not only to God's people but to the world. And here today as we begin the Keswick Convention, the beginning of the three weeks here, we are to declare the Lord is the Lord of the heavens and the earth who is in charge of history. This declaration is not just for us in this Keswick Convention. As you read Psalm 99 – 'The LORD reigns, let the nations tremble' – this phrase, this declaration, 'The LORD reigns' is not only for us but for the world.

Yesterday we had the invitation for people to stand up from different parts of the UK, from Scotland, Wales, even further away, from

Europe, from New Zealand. So, suddenly, we know that the Lord is
not a tribal God, not even a God of an international community.
When we declare, 'The LORD reigns,' we are declaring that God is the
God of the cosmos, the God of the heavens and the earth.

If you read from the book of Ephesians, this is what Paul says: 'he',
that is, God, 'raised him from the dead and seated him at his right hand
in the heavenly realms, far above all rule and authority, power and
dominion, and every title that can be given, not only in the present age
but also in the one to come. And God placed all things under his feet
and appointed him to be head over everything' (Eph. 1:20–22). The
Lord Jesus Christ reigns above all powers and authorities, in the past,
present and in the future and that's where we begin. Today we want to
declare that the Lord reigns. God is Sovereign. Live confidently.

As we come to Psalm 97 we come back to this question of God's
mission. We want to ask the question, 'For what purpose?' In your
Bible please turn to Psalm 97 because we'll be reading the text again
and again, examining and studying it together. I want to study this
psalm under three headings:

1. The call to holy fear – Christ is our King
2. The call to joyful worship – Christ is our Lord
3. The call to righteous living – Christ is our Judge

As we begin to read Psalm 97, you notice here in verses 2–4 there is
this picture of the power of nature, and three specific entities were
mentioned. First, the cloud and thick darkness; second, fire and third,
lightning. Of course, if you were an Israelite and you read this psalm
you would be familiar with this image of fire, lightning and clouds
picturing God's salvation. Let me just read to you part of Psalm 77. It
says here, 'The clouds poured down water, the skies resounded with
thunder; your arrows flashed back and forth. Your thunder was heard
in the whirlwind, your lightning lit up the world; the earth trembled
and quaked. Your path led through the sea, your way through the
mighty waters, though your footprints were not seen' (vv.17–19).
Psalm 77 depicted God's salvation in that picture of the lightning, the
fire and the water. God led the people of Israel out of Egypt.

But also these images of lightning, dark clouds and thunder reminded the people of God's holy presence. You are familiar with the account in Exodus 19 when the people had just come out of Egypt. As they came to the foot of the mountain, Mount Sinai, this is what it says in verse 16: 'On the morning of the third day there was thunder and lightning, with a thick cloud over the mountain'. Everyone trembled before God. Now, what follows is very important: 'The LORD descended to the top of Mount Sinai and called Moses to the top of the mountain . . . and the LORD said to him, "Go down and warn the people so they do not force their way through to see the LORD and many of them perish. Even the priests, who approach the LORD, must consecrate themselves . . . Put limits around the mountain and set it apart as holy"' (vv.20–22). Here we are reminded that the image of dark clouds and lightning reminds us of the importance of the fear of God. God reminds us that as we approach him, we approach the holy God.

Now, if you read the book of Acts we learn one of the marks of the early church was holy fear. If you read Acts 2, you are reminded that they met together in the temple court and in homes. And as they fellowshipped together they broke bread and listened to the Word of God. The phrase used here in chapter 2:43 is, 'everyone was filled with awe'. A-W-E, awe, alternatively translated as *fear*. Now, I work with OMF. There are many missionaries in OMF, formerly the China Inland Mission, some are young and some more senior people. I always have senior colleagues who come to me and complain. They say, 'Patrick, nowadays the younger people always abuse the word AWE. Everything is awesome – Disneyland is an awesome theme park. The word *awe* has been hijacked to be used for entertainment.' The word awe originally was only used for God, the fear of God.

One of the characteristics of the early church was that they feared God above everything else. You remember the story of John and Peter as they faced the leaders of the Sanhedrin. They commanded them not to speak in the name of Jesus. You remember their answer: 'Is it right for us to obey you or is it right for us to obey God?' (see Acts 4:19). Putting it in other words, 'Is it right for us to fear you more than fearing God?' You remember the story in Acts 4 when they were released from prison. They went back and had a prayer meeting, the first phrase from that prayer was, 'Sovereign Lord' (Acts 4:24).

We talk about God's mission tonight and throughout these few evenings. Mission is not necessarily something that we do for God; it's not as if we are doing God a favour. Mission is about obedience to the holy God, to fear God above everything else. And Paul picks up this idea of fearing God above everything else in Philippians 2. He says, 'Therefore God exalted him,' that is, Christ, 'to the highest place and gave him the name that is above every name, that at the name of Jesus every knee should bow, in heaven and on earth and under the earth, and every tongue confess that Jesus Christ is Lord' (vv.9–11). And then he says, 'Therefore, my dear friends . . . continue to work out your salvation with fear and trembling' (v.12). As we approach God we approach the holy God with fear.

Now, in his book *Rediscovering Holiness*, J.I. Packer says, 'Godly Christians have always been marked by a two-sided perception of holiness.' On the one hand, he explains, we are amazed by the transcendent glory of God's love; on the other hand, we stand in awe of the transcendent glory of God's sovereignty. God's love and God's sovereignty, God's mercy and the fear of God.

Yesterday many people stood up when we asked who was from Scotland. Now, you know that in 1924 there was the Paris Olympics. There were delegates from Britain and among the delegates there was one man from Scotland by the name of Eric Liddell. Many of you know the story. He was called 'the Flying Scotsman'. He ran so fast that many people believed that he would win gold in the Olympics. But when he arrived in Paris, he found out that he was supposed to run on Sunday and he refused to run. He felt that that was the day he wanted to worship God and so he told the Olympics committee that he would not run on Sunday. Of course, the committee was very disappointed and got angry with him. Even the Royal Family came to see him and said you should honour your nation by running on that day. He said, 'No, first I honour God; second I honour the nation. When I run, I run for the glory of God; when I run I feel the pleasure of God.' Of course, in the end the Olympic committee compromised and didn't make him run on Sunday but on Thursday instead.

Instead of running for 100 metres they got him to run for 400 metres, which he had never trained for. Many people wondered, 'How can he win, because he never trained for the 400 metres?' But in the end he not only won the gold medal, he broke the world record for that particular year. But at the peak of his career, one year after that, in 1925 he went to China and became a missionary. For the rest of his life he served God. He says, 'I ran for the glory of God.' Holy fear.

Secondly, we come to the *call to joyful worship*. Of course, we talk of the fear of God but we are not a bunch of Christians who are nervous, who are insecure, fearing judgement day. Psalm 97 gives us this wonderful picture of joyful worship. It says in verse 1, 'let the earth be glad; let the distant shores rejoice,' and in verse 8, 'Zion hears and rejoices and the villages of Judah are glad'. This is a picture of rejoicing together; there is this joyful worship. Many of you have had this experience of travelling in an aeroplane: the aeroplane went through a thunderstorm and the plane was shaking violently. How many of you have gone through that? You pray and when the plane lands usually you hear this loud clapping; people rejoice because the pilot landed the plane safely. Now there is this indescribable joy. Note: the Lord reigns in those thunderstorms, the pilot landed a plane safely and yet we are reminded here the Lord reigns. From Psalm 93 through to Psalm 99 there was this declaration that the Lord reigns and then Psalm 100 says, 'Shout for joy to the LORD, all the earth. Worship the LORD with gladness; come before him with joyful songs' (vv.1–2).

In many ways Christians are a very noisy bunch, rejoicing, praising God. We cannot keep quiet. Worship is tangible, it's visible, it's palpable, it's seen by others. In the context of Acts 2, you remember, the first believers worshipped God 'with sincere hearts' (v.46). They praised God and they enjoyed the favour of all the people (see v.47). Worship is not performance; worship is not pretence, and it's not a chore because worship is authentic. We are not only authentic with God, there is authenticity with one another and that draws people to turn to God. Here the psalmist is very clear. It's not just us worshipping; it's not just this tent here with three thousand people, worship always extends an invitation to others. It's not exclusive, because if you read Psalm 96, you will read this: 'Ascribe to the LORD, O families of nations, ascribe to the LORD glory and strength. Ascribe to the LORD the glory due to his name . . . Say among the nations, "The LORD reigns"' (vv.7–10). Say *among the nations* – there is always an invitation to others to join in worship together.

We know that we are on this pilgrimage of inviting others; we worship God by inviting others as well. I love the insightful comment Professor Andrew Walls, who is from Edinburgh, makes about invitation. He says there is a difference between the crusader mode and the missionary mode. A crusader may first issue an invitation but in the end he is prepared to compel, to force people to join. But he says the missionary is different. Even if his natural instinct is to decide compulsion he cannot compel but only demonstrate, invite, explain and leave the result with God. And the person who invites is one who is willing to live on terms set by other people – *to live on terms set by other people.*

The Word to the World – the Word is proclaimed to the world as we engage with the world and are willing to live on terms set by other people. And here we are not oblivious to the reality of the world because Psalm 97 says, 'All who worship images are put to shame' (v.7). There are many others who will not welcome this invitation and they will not roll out the red carpet for us. Many of us will face opposition and persecution. Increasingly, every time I visit the UK we are in a very post-Christian situation. And yet when I look at the Bible again I think of Silas and Paul in prison in Philippi. In the middle of the night they worshipped God with songs and singing. Can you imagine being in prison in the middle of the night? They were singing songs to God; that's the reality they faced.

Some of you know Pastor Wang Ming-Dao. He was a very famous pastor in China, very famous in preaching the Word of God faithfully. Because he was so faithful in preaching the Word of God he was imprisoned for many, many years. In the early 1980s when he was released from prison, the news got out and many visitors wanted to see him, including Billy Graham who came to visit him in China. When they visited him Pastor Dao always had this custom of inviting the visitors to join him in worshipping God with songs and the reading of the Word. But there was one problem, when Pastor Dao sang he sang so loud even the people down the road could hear him and the visitors were very nervous. They'd say, 'Shhhhh! You were just released from prison, be quiet.' And he would say, 'I worshipped God in prison. I sang. And now I worship God when I am free, I sing all the more with joy!' There is joyful worship. We cannot stop worshipping God with a joyful heart.

And finally, it's the *call to righteous living.* The Bible is very clear that joyful worship needs to be translated into righteous living. It's not just singing here together, but your daily activities. Last year I attended the Lausanne Congress in Cape Town with four thousand brothers and sisters from all over the world. There was this tremendous, indescribable experience of worshipping God together for seven days. A glimpse of heaven, you know, all tribes, nations and tongues worship God together. And yet I'm reminded again, it's not just seven days of being together, but in my daily walk I serve the righteous God. If you read Psalm 97 very carefully, from verse one all the way to the end the psalmist reminds us again that we are serving a righteous God.

Verse 2: 'Clouds and thick darkness surround him; righteousness and justice are the foundation of his throne.' Verse 6: 'The heavens proclaim his righteousness, and all the peoples see his glory.' Verse 10: 'Let those who love the LORD hate evil'. Verse 11: 'Light is shed upon the righteous'. Verse 12: 'Rejoice in the LORD, you who are righteous, and praise his holy name.' The psalmist in Psalm 97 reminds us again that joyful worship must be translated into righteous living.

You remember the story of Joseph? In Genesis 39 Joseph says, when he faced seduction from Potiphar's wife – and I like the way it is described in the Bible in verses 9–10: 'How then could I do such a wicked thing and sin against God? . . . he refused to go to bed with her *or even be with her*' (emphasis mine). This phrase really just struck me, '*or even be with her*'. How often do we guard our boundary in order to serve a righteous God? To guard our boundary! You remember the story of Joseph's brothers? They were very afraid that Joseph may retaliate when his father died and yet Joseph said this, 'God intended it for good to accomplish what is now being done, the saving of many lives' (Genesis 50:20). And Joseph twice says, 'God sent me ahead of you' (see Genesis 45:5,7). There was no bitterness. In God's sovereign rule Joseph accepted what God allowed him to go through. We serve a righteous God, 'How then shall we live?' May I change it to, 'How then shall we walk?' Because Paul in Ephesians, actually seven times, said, 'This is the way you should walk', or 'This is the way you should not walk.' Walking is an applicable metaphor for our way of life.

I mentioned about the Cape Town commitment at the Lausanne Congress last year. At the end of the Lausanne Congress, there was a book published called *The Cape Town Commitment*. It speaks about righteous living or biblical living. It says that the world is right to ask if our Christian faith makes any difference at all, if there is no distinction in conduct between non-Christians and Christians. Does our Christian faith make any difference at all? Our message carries no authenticity to a watching world. There is no biblical mission without biblical living. There's a Chinese proverb that says, 'There's a lot of thunder, but no rain.' There's a lot of noise, there's a lot of speaking but nothing showing in our lives. And I think the world is watching whether we carry our message with authenticity. At the end of that booklet, *The Cape Town Commitment*, it challenges God's people to walk in humility, in integrity, in simplicity. Now, Chris Wright will be our speaker next week and he uses an acronym: H – I – S. We are his; we belong to Christ; that means walking in humility, integrity and simplicity.

I would like to end by just telling you this story. It's a real story in the history of the Mission in China. Many of you know about the Boxer Rebellion in 1900. It was one of the most difficult periods for missionaries. In that one year thousands of Christians died. Of course, not just Chinese Christians but many missionaries died because of the Boxer Rebellion. In the China Inland Mission, fifty-eight missionaries died including twenty-two children. Those of you who have read the record will know that many of the children died because they were beheaded. They chopped off their heads, that's how brutal it was. When the dust finally settled and the Chinese government decided to compensate these missionaries for what they lost, the China Inland Mission leaders came together. As they prayed, they decided to accept no compensation for lives lost, for bodily injury or the loss of property. This was a real shock to the Chinese government. They said,

'Why do you not ask for compensation?' And this was their reply, 'We came with the good news; we were willing to even give our lives for the sake of the Chinese people, for the sake of the gospel.' This really struck the Chinese government and the Governor of Shanxi Provence wrote a letter. He said, 'I want this letter to be hung on every wall of government offices, in schools, in offices and places, and I want it to be read out to others,' and this is what he wrote: 'I charge you all, scholars, army and lay people, those of you who are fathers, to exhort your sons, those of you who are elder sons, to exhort your younger brothers, to bear in mind the example of the China Inland Mission who is able to forbear and forgive as taught by Jesus Christ.' He says, 'Jesus, in his instruction, inculcates forbearance and forgiveness, and all the desire for revenge is discouraged. The China Inland Mission is able to carry out these principles to the full and this mode of action deserves our attention.' It says, 'These people follow the example of Jesus Christ. They are followers of Christ, their message carries authenticity.'

I want to close. Just to summarize: here in Psalm 97 we find three things. First, the *call to holy fear*: we acknowledge Christ is King. Mission is about obedience, not so much about activities. Second, the *call to joyful worship*: we acknowledge Christ is Lord. We invite others to join us as well, even though there may be times of difficulties and suffering. And third, the *call to righteous living*: we acknowledge Christ as Judge. He will come back; he will return and judge the world. There is no biblical mission without biblical living and I pray - I pray for myself and I pray for you too wherever you may be, wherever you may go back to - 'Lord, help us to walk with humility, Lord, help us to walk with integrity, and Lord, help us to walk with simplicity.' Yes, we declare, 'The Lord reigns.' The Lord is in charge. Amen.

In whose name?

By Amy Orr-Ewing

Amy Orr-Ewing

Amy Orr-Ewing is the UK Director for RZIM Europe and Curriculum Director for the Oxford Centre for Christian Apologetics. She has written a number of books and is a regular columnist for *Christianity* magazine, as well as speaking and lecturing on Christian Apologetics worldwide. Amy lives in Buckinghamshire with her husband Frog and their three boys where they have recently planted a new church called the Latimer Minster.

In whose name? John 9:24–39

In these evenings we have been thinking about God's mission, and tonight we are going to be looking at this question, 'In whose name?' As I was driving here on Friday I was rather amazed to read in a newspaper the headline, 'New pupils who don't even know their name.' We are told that a growing number of children are starting school or nursery in Britain not knowing their own name and not knowing what a name is. The newspaper article tells us parents who spend too much time on the internet and watching television are failing to teach children how to speak. In the worst cases children reach the age of four unaware that they even have a name! Toddlers should be familiar with their own name by the age of two, teachers say. 'It was very upsetting to realize that children reach the age of four without that difficulty being picked up,' one teacher said. We do have a problem and anecdotally it's getting worse. In about ten per cent of cases, parents were not to blame because their children had language or communication difficulties caused by disabilities, but the remainder could be avoided by families spending more time together. Isn't that staggering?

As we gather here tonight at Keswick and think about what it means to go out on mission in somebody's name we are reminded that we are living in a country where a generation are growing up, many of whom don't even know what a name is. What is a name? A name is so much; it gives humanity and dignity to a person. We are told by historians that nineteenth-century London was such a time of spiritual, emotional and material poverty and children were so utterly uncared for that some were even without names. They were known to each other by nicknames or by numbers. You see, a godless culture loses the value of human life. If there's no vision in a culture for the idea of human beings created in the image of God, if there's only survival of the fittest or karma, people become nameless commodities.

Names carry meanings in the Bible. They denote something of the character, the destiny and the nature of the person. And so when we ask this question, 'In whose name?' we are asking a radical question in our generation, a question that sets the Christian faith apart from its rivals because we go as Christians in the name of a personal God, who makes himself known, who enters space, time and history in the person of Christ. It's in his name that we go.

In Acts 4:7–11 after Peter and John have just healed a crippled man we read, 'They had Peter and John brought before them and began to question them: "By what power or what name did you do this?" Then Peter, filled with the Holy Spirit, said to them: "Rulers and elders of the people! If we are being called to account today for an act of kindness shown to a cripple and are asked how he was healed, then know this, you and all the people of Israel: It is by the name of Jesus Christ of Nazareth, whom you crucified but whom God raised from the dead, that this man stands before you healed . . . Salvation is found in no one else, for there is no other name under heaven given to men by which we must be saved."'

Do you see the power of the name of Jesus? There is no other name under heaven or on earth by which anybody can be saved other than by the name of Jesus. And yet today it is highly controversial to make such a unique claim. Can it really be only through Jesus that people are saved? Isn't that intolerant? Isn't that arrogant? Isn't that discriminatory?

In our passage tonight Jesus asks the man who he had healed and who had become the centre of religious dispute a profound question. You know, in the gospels Jesus asks over 157 questions and every single one of them is profound. In John's gospel alone, he asks more than thirty questions, depending on how you translate some of the things Jesus said. And tonight we are going to examine one of these questions: 'Jesus heard that they had thrown him out, and when he found him, he said, "Do you believe in the Son of Man?"' (9:35). Do you believe in the Son of Man? Now, in order to understand the question that Jesus is asking here we need to flip back in our Bibles to Daniel 7:13–14 where the nature of the Son of Man is described for us in prophetic brilliance by Daniel. 'In my vision at night I looked, and there before me was one like a son of man, coming with the clouds of heaven. He approached the Ancient of Days and was led into his presence. He was given authority, glory and sovereign power; all peoples, nations and men of every language worshipped him. His dominion is an everlasting dominion that will not pass away, and his kingdom is one that will never be destroyed.'

Here Jesus is talking to a man whom he healed and he asks him a question, 'Do you believe in the Son of Man?' I believe he asks us that question today in twenty-first-century Britain. What does it mean to believe in the Son of Man? Well, we are told in Daniel that the Son of Man comes on the clouds of heaven, that the Son of Man is a person who can approach the covenant God, the Eternal God, the Ancient of Days. We are told that the Son of Man has authority, glory and sovereign power. He is divine and he has the ability to judge the world. And we are told all peoples of every language will worship him. We are told that his dominion is everlasting.

Here's the question: 'Do you believe in the Son of Man?' In other words, do you believe in Jesus as the one who approaches the Ancient of Days, who will come on the clouds of heaven in glory, who has sovereign power, who will judge the world? Do you believe in Jesus as the one whom all peoples, whatever their tribal ethnicity or geographical context is, should worship? Do you believe that peoples of every language, whatever their culture or religion might be, should worship him? Do you believe that Jesus is not a tribal God for one group of people, but he is for all peoples? And do you believe that his reign is everlasting; it's not just for a particular period in time? Do you believe in Jesus in this kind of way? Do you believe that he is God? That he has authority and glory and power. Do you believe that he will judge all people? Do you believe that he is the God of the universe for all people groups and that he is everlasting? What a question! It's a humbling question that we are asked to consider tonight.

In February I had the privilege of preaching in Istanbul in Turkey. I was involved in a public evangelistic event as well as preaching in the church. I was overwhelmed by the situation of the church in that country. There are over 70 million people living in Turkey and between maybe two and four thousand evangelicals. Imagine that, living in a country of 70 million people and the size of the evangelical church is similar to the crowd sitting in this room today. That's it! There are no other evangelical Christians. I was preaching on some of the questions in John's gospel and this was one of them: 'Do you believe in the Son of Man?' Do you believe that Jesus is the one who should be worshipped by every tribe and language and people and nation including the Turkish people, even when you are a tiny minority? Do you really believe in Jesus as the Son of Man? If you do, this will shape how you live. If Jesus really is the one who will come on the clouds of heaven and judge the world, how desperately we need his salvation. And doesn't his very name Jesus mean *salvation*, the one who will save people from their sins?

God didn't send us a scientist, an economist or an entertainer. Our greatest need was for forgiveness, so God sent us a Saviour. God sent us Jesus, the one who saves. So in whose name do we go? We go in the name of Jesus, the Son of Man, the Saviour and the Judge of the world.

But do we actually believe this? Let alone go in his name. We can think we are going and living with purpose and so easily get lulled into living in practice without intention and without passion for the name of Jesus. It's so easy to forget him, to get on with life without him and live like everyone else around us. Theoretically, we believe in the Son of Man but practically we live as atheists. We don't go at all, let alone in anyone's name. Why is that the case? Well, I believe we face a massive challenge, the challenge of truth, and I want to explore that for a few moments. Why is it that although we, theoretically, in a church meeting can say, 'Yes, I believe, Lord Jesus, that you are the Son of Man,' why is it that we don't live that out?

Towards the end of the last government, one of the ministers invited a group of Christian leaders to come to Westminster to discuss how they had done as a government from the perspective of faith leaders. We met in one of the cabinet rooms and were talking about the church's perspective on some of the legislation that had happened in the previous thirteen years. As the meeting got going the minister in charge began, 'I want to welcome you all here today as Christian leaders. We as the government want to hear how we've done; we think it's really important to engage with the faith communities. Today we are going to hear from you Christians and next week we have got the Muslim leaders coming in, and the week after that we have got the Hindu leaders coming in because we believe it's really important to listen to people of faith.' Fascinating! Right there in that sentence the minister who had intended to complement the church had relativized the truth of Jesus Christ as just another faith like all the faiths.

Why might we sit here in this tent tonight and be able to say to Jesus, 'Yes, I believe that you are the Son of Man,' but as soon as we get out of those doors we struggle to speak about him? Why? Because faith has come to mean something that the Bible doesn't define it as in our culture. Richard Dawkins defines faith as belief in something despite all the evidence to the contrary. He says, 'You know you require faith to believe what you believe because there's no evidence, there are no reasons; if there are reasons, you wouldn't need faith.' How different from biblical faith. We trust in the God who is actually there and who makes himself known. But in the face of pluralism we can feel that we are on the back foot, that if we speak for Jesus Christ we will look silly.

Ravi Zacharias, my boss, says that in the West many people like to believe that all religions are fundamentally the same but just superficially different, whereas in reality they are just superficially similar but fundamentally different. Why, as Christians, do we struggle to speak about Jesus as the only way? Well, I want to suggest tonight that there are three reasons that we struggle to do that. First, is that we feel somehow we would be intolerant and nobody British wants to be intolerant. But what does tolerance mean? A dictionary definition tells us, 'Tolerance is the willingness to accept or tolerate somebody or something especially opinions or behaviour that you may not agree with or people who are not like you.' Tolerance has come to be defined as agreement to say, 'Yes, Jesus is great, Christianity is great but so is Islam and so is Hinduism and all the faiths are great and I am a tolerant person.' That's not what tolerance means. Tolerance is respect for somebody you do not agree with. In other words, it is only because I disagree with my Muslim Imam friend about the status of Jesus Christ that I need to tolerate him, to practice love and tolerance.

Well, the second problem we face is that we fear we will sound arrogant. If I say, 'Jesus is the only name under heaven by which we can be saved. Jesus you are the Son of Man, you are the one who will judge the world, who people of every tribe and language and nation and tongue must worship,' if I live as if I believe that, I'll be an arrogant person. Wouldn't I? You know, I couldn't possibly be the person that says other people are wrong, that would make me arrogant, wouldn't it?'

The story is often told of the elephant and the blind scribes. It's actually from the Hindu scriptures, this story. The blind scribes are standing around the different parts of the elephant and one is holding the tail of the elephant, and he says, 'It's a rope.' Somebody else is holding the leg of the elephant and he says, 'No, you're wrong; it's not a rope, it's a tree trunk,' and somebody else is holding the trunk of the elephant and says, 'You're both wrong; it's not a tree trunk, it's not a rope, it's a snake.' This is a parable of the different religions of the world. They all have a piece of the elephant; if only they would not be so arrogant as to say it is only their truth that is the truth. Ever heard that story?

But what is the difference between the person telling the story and the people inside the story? The person telling the story can see and has the big picture of ultimate reality; the elephant, and the people inside the picture are blind and they cannot see the wood for the trees. They are up close to the elephant, so what they are saying is Jesus, Buddha, Krishna, Mohammed, Moses are the same. They are all blind but me, aged 19, at university, I can see. I can see the whole of reality. Here is the question, who is arrogant? Isn't it just as arrogant to say that you know all faiths will lead to God as it is to say, 'I agree with Jesus when he claimed to be the Son of Man?'

Well, then, you might say, 'Aren't we discriminating when we say it's only Jesus, that Jesus is the Son of Man. Wouldn't that make us discriminatory to live not as practical atheists but as practical believers in Jesus the Son of Man?' A number of years ago my husband Frog was pastoring a church in inner city London and we were doing lots of youth ministry amongst children from the gangs and young people from the streets in that community. A number of large trust funds heard about the work we were doing and wanted to financially support the ministry in this poor area. One lady came representing a trust fund; she observed the work and she liked the social work side of it but she did not like the Jesus proclamation that went alongside it. She said to my husband, 'I'd like to give you money' – we were talking about between fifteen and twenty thousand pounds a year – 'but I'd seek assurances from you that you would not seek to proselytize people of other faiths.' So my husband Frog said, 'I'm very sorry; I could not give you that assurance as, you see, Jesus Christ is central to all that we do here.' And then he said, 'In fact, in this church we don't believe in discrimination and I couldn't accept money if you were trying to get me to be discriminatory.' She looked worried. She said, 'What do you mean? I don't believe in discrimination either.' And he said, 'We do not discriminate against anybody on the basis of their nationality, their language, their colour, their people group; we tell everybody the same message about Jesus. We don't discriminate against anyone on the basis of their religion because we believe Jesus is for everyone.'

'Do you believe in the Son of Man?' Jesus asked the man born blind this question in John 9 and he asks us this question today. The man said, 'Who is he, sir? Tell me so that I may believe in him.' Fascinating! And Jesus said, 'You have now seen him; in fact, he is the one speaking with you.' And the man said, ' "Lord, I believe," and he worshipped him' (vv.36–38). 'Do you believe in the Son of Man?' That's the question I believe Jesus asks you today.

In whose name? We go in the name of Jesus, the one who is the Son of Man, the one who is the only Saviour of the world, the one who is the only name under heaven by which anybody can be saved. But do you know what? People need to be told about that in order to be able to believe in him. What a challenge out of the mouth of an unbeliever! 'Tell me, so that I may believe in him.' Let that challenge ring out in your hearts as you think about where you are going back to after the Keswick Convention.

'Do you believe in the Son of Man?' If we believe that Jesus is the one who is to be worshipped by all, who will judge the world and who is the only one who can save us, it will affect how we live. It will enable us to overcome those challenges about feeling we are being intolerant. We won't be intolerant because we can speak about him in a way that respects people who disagree. We can overcome that fear we might be arrogant. We don't have to be arrogant at all. It is just as arrogant to say that Jesus is not the way. We can overcome the fear that somehow we might be discriminatory. Let's not discriminate against anyone. Let's tell the world about this Son of Man. If we believe that Jesus is the one who is to be worshipped it will affect how we live.

Recently I had the privilege of doing some ministry in a communist country and speaking to leaders of the underground church. I was involved in doing some training in apologetics and trying to help and equip Christian leaders to speak about God in public and take on some of the communist ideologies. And after one of the meetings a lady came to me and said, 'I have a question for you and I need to know the answer to this question.' She began to tell the story about how she and her husband had been leading a network of churches that was growing very quickly. Every day people were coming to know Jesus but one day the authorities came. They broke into her house and they took her husband away. Her child was a year old, she had no means of support, and she had concern for all these churches. For months she did not know what had happened to her husband and she had to somehow continue to try and support her child and this ministry. And she said, 'Here's my question. Should I pray for my husband to be released?' She said, 'Don't answer it yet; let me tell you more. After six months the communist authorities let me know where my husband was being held and I was able to go and visit him in prison. I went to visit him in prison and, as we spoke, he told me of how he had led the prison warden to Christ and sixty per cent of the prison was now attending his Sunday service in jail.' And she said, 'Is it right for me to pray for him to be released because I so desperately need him at home, or should he stay where he is in that place of fruitfulness?'

Only somebody who believes in Jesus as the Son of Man could even ask that question, and my reaction to that question challenged me to the core. I say that I believe this but do I live as someone who believes in Jesus as the only name under heaven by which we can be saved? What about the recent converts to Christianity from amongst the ranks of the Taliban? There's a wonderful work of God going on in Afghanistan and Northern Pakistan with ex-Talibans coming to know Jesus Christ, and within weeks going on mission and preaching trips and handing out Bibles. One young man who had been a Christian for two weeks was attacked by a mob as he preached about Jesus. He was hung up by his hair and tortured. He managed to escape but had two circular bald patches where his hair had been wrenched from his head. But you know what his testimony was? 'Where are we going next week? Which village are we going to preach in next week? Jesus is the Son of Man, the cost is worth paying.' Do you believe in the Son of Man? Are we known as believers or are we in deep cover? In our workplaces, communities and families, are we prepared to rise up with courage and take his name to a dying world?

One of my favourite writers, C.T. Studd, put it like this: 'Let us not glide through the world and then slip quietly into heaven without having blown the trumpet long and loud for our Redeemer, Jesus Christ. Let us see to it that the devil will hold a thanksgiving service in hell when he gets the news of our departure from the fields of battle.' Wouldn't it be great if the devil threw a party when you died?

Jesus asks the man, 'Do you believe in the Son of Man?' Do you believe in Jesus as the one who came in history, the Saviour of the world, who at the cross took the sins of this broken, dying, evil, sick world upon himself so that we could be forgiven? In whose name do we go? Let it be in Jesus' name. And let us go in confidence and grace, with courage and love, with conviction and passion. Let us go in his name. Amen.

With what message?

BBC Radio 4 service

For a number of years one of the Convention evening celebration services has been recorded and later broadcast by BBC Radio 4. This year the recording took place on 19 July during the first week of the Convention. The following interviews and sermon give a flavour of the service but for reasons of space the songs, prayers and Bible readings have been omitted.

With what message? Romans 5:1–8

Leader: Welcome to the Keswick Convention in the heart of the English Lake District. Now stretching over three weeks each summer, the annual Convention – hosted in the beautiful town of Keswick – welcomes some twelve thousand Christians from across the denominations, from many different countries, and from all age groups. And for over 130 years this annual event has gathered Christians to hear God's Word through the Bible, to celebrate his goodness in worship, and to commit ourselves to serve Christ more fully. Our theme this year is the *Word to the World*. Throughout the week we are looking at how God's Word is at work in our lives, our nation and around the globe.

Across the country this year there have been various celebrations marking the 400th anniversary of the King James Bible. Here is what one of many famous people has said, 'You can't appreciate English literature unless you are to some extent steeped in the King James Bible. Not to know the King James Bible is to be, in some small way, a barbarian.' These supportive words are from Richard Dawkins, and there have been many similar. Most have tended to highlight its influence on language and culture. Joan Bakewell declared the King James to be 'one of the greatest works of literature ever written'.

And whilst these statements are true, I sometimes wonder what Moses, Jeremiah or Paul would have said to such praise. Someone once suggested it would be rather like picking up the original manuscript of

Einstein's *Theory of Relativity* and to say, 'What beautiful handwriting!' There is much more to God's Word than its literary legacy, remarkable though that is. Some years ago a man called J.B. Phillips was working on a paraphrase of the Bible and explained that the experience was similar to working on the mains electricity of a house, but doing so with the electricity still switched on. It was an electric experience: the book was *live*, it was powerful and energizing.

Paul explains this when he writes to the Thessalonians, 'And we also thank God continually because, when you received the word of God, which you heard from us, you accepted it not as the word of men, but as it actually is, the word of God which is at work in you who believe' (1 Thess. 2:13). God's Word is authoritative and powerful and at work today. In today's service we rejoice in that word of the gospel which is advancing across the globe.

One of our guests at Keswick this year is Dr Helen Roseveare. Her previous visit to this event nearly forty years ago was highly memorable, as Dr Roseveare described her missionary experience in the Congo. Since then she has travelled worldwide proclaiming the gospel and through her books, her teaching and her example, is encouraging Christians everywhere to commit themselves to the cause of Christian mission.

Leader: Welcome, Helen. Please tell us first something of your upbringing.

H.R.: I was brought up in a happy, normal, middle class family. We were basically church-going but with no real understanding of the meaning of the gospel. I went up to Cambridge University in the last year of World War Two.

Leader: How did you become a career missionary?

H.R.: There were Christian girls at university who made friends with me, and helped me to settle in to this very new environment. Their lifestyle, integrity, and generous friendliness created in me a hunger to know what made them different from others. Slowly, they introduced me to the Lord Jesus Christ, the Son of God, and I began to learn the facts of the gospel – that God's Son died for me on Calvary that I might know forgiveness of sins and be given a real purpose for my life. Overwhelmed that the Lord both knew me and so loved me that he was willing to die for me, I cried out to him for forgiveness of my sins. And God met with me and I fell in love with Jesus that evening. You could say that this love took over my life. My ambition from that moment was to tell others of the love of God – anywhere, every-where, under any circumstances.

Leader: We know something of the personal cost over these sixty years of service since you were first called to serve the Lord Jesus. Was it worth it?

H.R.: Humanly, the cost could be thought of as leaving family, changing cultures, having to learn a new language, loneliness, an overwhelming sense of inadequacy, and then eventually five months as a captive of guerrilla soldiers – beaten, terrified, raped – before I was rescued. But never have I regretted responding to God's call to serve him – anywhere, everywhere, under any circumstances. I love him more than ever and trust by his grace to continue to love and serve him to the end of my days as he enables me.

Leader: We are also delighted to have two Asian Christian leaders with us this week: Dr Ajith Fernando from Sri Lanka, who will speak to us shortly, and Dr Patrick Fung from Singapore, the General Director of the Overseas Missionary Fellowship. Patrick, could you tell us a little about your background?

P.F.: I was born in Hong Kong from a traditional Chinese family. I am a medical doctor by training, first in Australia then in the UK. I became a Christian when I was a medical student in Australia. In 1989, my wife, Jennie, who is also a medical doctor, and I went to Pakistan and served in a local hospital for about seven years. That was a wonderful time though with many challenges. We appreciated the deep friendship with the local people and our neighbours. They were often interested to find out why we came to serve them. They were also curious to know why Chinese could be Christians. Often the local people's concept of Christianity is that it is a Western religion. They were surprised to know that there are many Christians in China today.

Leader: Can you give us a brief summary of how the Christian gospel is advancing in Asia?

P.F.: More than 100 years ago, at the 1910 Edinburgh Conference, there was the vision to bring the gospel to the non-Christian areas, from the West to the rest of the world. Today, the world is very different. Asia has seen some of the most significant church growth in the world today. In Korea, more than thirty per cent of the population professes to be Christians. Korea has sent out more than twenty thousand cross-cultural missionaries in the year 2010 and this figure keeps increasing. It is difficult to estimate accurately the exact number of Christians in China, but a conservative estimate puts the figure at least at 50 million.

One time, a foreigner was attending a church service in Beijing. The sermon could be quite long in a Chinese church, ranging from one hour to an hour and a half. This foreigner noticed a very interesting phenomenon. Many who attended the morning service stayed back for the second service, and many who attended the second service stayed back for the third service even though the sermon was the same. This foreigner asked some of the local people why they would stay for the second service even though the message was the same. They replied, 'It is the Word of God. We want to hear it again!' No wonder the church is growing.

We have seen revivals in other places too, including India and Burma, for example. In India, often these revival meetings are held in the open air when thousands of people gather to hear the Word preached for a whole week or ten days. The facilities are very limited and many have to travel for days to get there. But there is a deep spiritual hunger for the Word of God. I know of three Mongolian pastors who travelled on the train for three days to get to a Bible conference where they could hear the Word of God. I spoke at a Christian medical students' conference in Indonesia up in the mountains when four hundred medical students gathered together to hear the Word of God. Many of them had travelled several days, by sea, land and bus to come to hear the Word of God. They started their first meeting every morning at 6 a.m.! The preaching of the Word brings a profound impact on the lives of many in Asia.

Not only are we seeing church growth, but we are also seeing mission movements across continents and across ethnic groups. I have witnessed Japanese Christians serving humbly among Chinese people and Chinese Christians serving in Japan in the earthquake-stricken area. The power of the gospel, with the cross as the central message, breaks down barriers of hostility and brings healing to past hurts and wounds. I see a new community that crosses ethnic, political boundaries, actively serving others. The gospel cannot be just proclaimed, but must be lived out in word and deed.

Leader: What do you think is most needed on the part of the Christian church in its task of mission?

P.F.: Perhaps many from the West are concerned about the persecuted church in Asia. However, persecution is not the biggest threat to the church in Asia or, may I say, anywhere. It is a diluted gospel that is the biggest threat to the church. It is a gospel that does not embrace suffering that is the biggest threat. For the cross is central to the Christian faith. Being willing to suffer is the acid test of the authenticity of our Christian faith. Many believers in Asia or other continents live in the midst of suffering as the cost of bearing witness to Christ in a hostile environment. We also face the danger of embracing a prosperity gospel – a gospel that equates wealth and success as a measure of our spirituality, a gospel that promotes a lifestyle and practices that are often unethical and un-Christlike. A church leader in China said to me, 'Do not give us money. Money will divide the church.' Perhaps the greatest need on the part of the Christian church in its task of mission is holiness, with integrity before God and integrity before men. Otherwise there will just be growth without depth. We do not want church growth that is miles wide and an inch deep. Persecution and suffering have purified the church in Asia, not destroyed it.

Leader: Ajith Fernando is the Director of Youth for Christ in Sri Lanka, but travels widely in Asia and beyond, teaching the Bible and explaining the good news of Jesus Christ. He speaks to us this morning from Romans 5 about the heart of the Christian message.

A.F.: I shall never forget a conversation I had with one of our drug rehabilitation workers. He himself had been a drug dependant and had served time in several of Sri Lanka's prisons. He told me that when he reads Paul, he thinks that Paul must have been a drug dependant at some time. What he wrote was so relevant to the struggles of a drug dependant that he also must have had that experience. He referred, for example, to the way Paul describes the believer's struggle with sin in Romans 7 where he says, 'I do not do the good I want, but the evil that I do not want is what I do' (see v. 19). He was talking about the oppressive battle with temptation which is very similar to the struggle a drug dependant has with addiction. Now, I don't believe for one minute that Paul was a drug dependant but I was struck by the fact that my colleague found the Christian message so relevant to his life.

The idea of a distant God bellowing an irrelevant message to an uninterested world won't stand when you realize that the primary way in which the voice of God is heard is through the life and work of Jesus Christ. For Paul, the key to the Christian message is, 'Jesus Christ and him crucified.' He knew that this message that Jesus Christ died for the sins of the world was not palatable to most people. In fact, he described it as a stumbling block to Jews and foolishness to the Gentiles. Yet he spoke of this message of the death of Christ as something that was powerful and appealing. In Romans 5:1-8 Paul draws out the implications of the death of Christ.

In verses 1 and 2 Paul talks about the consequences that flow from the death of Jesus Christ. He says, 'we have peace with God through our Lord Jesus Christ'. That means that we are no longer God's enemies, we can be his friends. Then Paul says that we have access to God.

This, then, is the primary benefit to us of the work of Christ: a relationship with our Creator where he treats us as his own children.

Then we come to verses 6–8 which brings us to the heart of the gospel, the good news of Christ. Paul says in verse 6 that 'while we were still weak, at the right time Christ died for the ungodly' (ESV). Despite all our achievements as humans, when it comes to living a righteous life, we fail, or as Paul says, 'We are weak.' This is because we have broken our ties with God, our Creator, and this has made us forfeit what God wished for us to have in order to be authentically human. Paul says that of our own efforts we cannot come out of this predicament. We stand guilty before God, deserving of his punishment, and then Paul says in verse 8, 'God shows his love for us in that while we were still sinners, Christ died for us' (ESV).

I was once speaking to a small group of people about the death of Christ and there was a lady there to whom this message seemed very strange. Her reaction was similar to the reaction of a lot of people when they are told that Jesus died for them: 'How could someone else die for me, how could someone else be punished for the wrong I've done? If any one should be punished shouldn't it be me?' This lady had a son with a marked limp because he had contracted polio when he was a little boy. I asked her, 'When your son was very sick did anyone think it was unfair or strange that you stayed up night after night making tremendous personal sacrifices in order to care for him?' 'Well,' she said, 'no.' Then I told her, 'That's what our Creator did for us. When he saw our hopeless condition he sent his Son to make the supreme sacrifice for us.' After the meeting this lady told a colleague of mine she now understood the message of the death of Christ.

Actually, the idea of one dying for another is not as strange as it seems at first. This is a principle that is ploughed into the facts of life on earth. We see it in our blood as the white blood cells go out to seek infection and sometimes they will die to rid us of this infection. In fact, the yellow pus that comes out of our wounds is the corpses of the white blood corpuscles that have died to rid us of infection. A mother bird will come in front of a snake that is coming to devour her baby birds and she dies to save the lives of those baby birds. We regard as heroes soldiers who die to protect the sovereignty of their nation. Similarly in Romans 5, Paul is saying that the spotless Son of God took our place; we had no hope of escaping the consequences of our wrongdoing so he took it on himself.

There was an old Chinese scholar who, when he heard for the first time the story that God had sent his Son to die for our sins, turned to his neighbours and said, 'Didn't I tell you that there ought to be a God like this?' The cross agrees with our deepest instincts of what the Creator God should do in the face of human need, or as Paul put it, 'God shows his love for us in that while we were still sinners, Christ died for us' (Rom. 5:8, ESV). If sacrificial love for the needy is a supreme human characteristic and if God is love, we would expect him to make him the supreme sacrifice to get us out of our mess.

You know, at the start of my talk I talked about my colleague who works with drug dependants. He was once, for some unknown reason, assaulted by a youth from the village that surrounds our drug rehabilitation centre. The moment I heard about this I went to meet him. And the first thing he told me was, 'Now I know that I am a Christian.' He explained to me that there were some students at the drug centre who wanted to hit back at these people; they wanted to go and assault them in return. My colleague stopped them and he was shocked at what he had done because he himself had been a gang leader and hitting back was normal for him, but now he had no desire for revenge. He said that when he was walking back to the Centre after the assault he felt an intensity of love and joy inside of him that he had never felt before. He knew that God was with him. God had proved his love by sending Jesus to die for him and he saw the reality of this when he was being assaulted.

This conviction drives us to proclaim the message of Jesus throughout the world. Earlier on in this same passage in verse 5 Paul said, 'God's love has been poured into our hearts through the Holy Spirit who has been given to us' (ESV). And that's what my colleague experienced as he was going back after the assault. Having experienced such love we are motivated to tell others about it. So Christians from all continents are united in this desire to proclaim this message to the world. We long for everyone to know this good news that God proves his love for us in that while we were still sinners Christ died for us.

Leader: Thank you for joining us. Why not come to Keswick next summer to enjoy the lakes and mountains, the Convention programme, and the English weather . . .

We close our service in prayer:

We thank you, Father, that the life which we now live in Christ, who died and rose again, is that life which is eternal. And the fellowship which we have in him unites us with your whole church on earth and in heaven. We pray that as we journey through the years and across the world, we may proclaim Christ the Saviour and serve Christ the King and, at the last, come to that abiding city where you reign for evermore. And now, may the grace of the Lord Jesus Christ, the love of God, and the fellowship of the Holy Spirit, be with us and all of God's people around the world now and for ever, Amen.

With whose resources?

By Tim Chester

Tim Chester

Tim Chester is a leader of The Crowded House, a church planting network in the UK and Australia. He is a co-director of The Porterbrook Network and the Northern Training Institute, as well as a prolific author. He has co-written the workbooks, *Gospel-Centred Church*, *Gospel-Centred Life*, *Gospel-Centred Family* and *Gospel-Centred Marriage* and is the series editor of *The Good Book Guides*. He is married with two daughters.

With whose resources?
Acts 1:1–8, 4:23–31

Let me tell you what happens to me every morning. My wife is a teacher and I have two teenage daughters. So the girls in my life leave the house in the morning to go off to school, usually by 8 o'clock hopefully, if we can get the slightly dawdling one out the door. By 8 o'clock I'm left on my own. And my plan, the notion I have in my head anyway, is that my working day should start at 9 o'clock. So I have an hour, from 8 o'clock to 9 o'clock that I will give to reading God's Word and prayer. My plan is I have an hour for prayer each morning.

In Acts 6 when there is that problem with the distribution of food the apostles appoint the seven so that they can give themselves to the ministry of God's Word and to prayer. I think that probably means half my job is praying, so an hour in the morning doesn't seem a bad place to start. But this is how it goes: at some point between 8 o'clock and 9 o'clock – on a good day it might be about twenty to nine but some days it's ten past and some days I never quite get going – at some point between 8 o'clock and 9 o'clock I start thinking about the work I've got to do and I stop thinking about praying. I think part of the problem is that I usually pray in my study. I sit in my armchair and opposite me is my desk with my computer on so I can see the list of jobs that I need to do. I start thinking about how important they are and

I need to get up and get on with them. I start to wonder what emails there are waiting for me and I think maybe if I could just get those emails out the way I'd feel better about my start to the day. Or I start to think about some talk I'm preparing; I have a great idea and I think, 'I just need to go over and just write that down,' and at some point between 8 o'clock and 9 o'clock each day, I stop praying and I get up and go over to my desk.

As I say, on a good day, that can be twenty to, quarter to nine but often it's sort of ten past, quarter past. At some point each morning I decide that my work is more important than God's work. At some point between 8 o'clock and 9 o'clock each day I decide that my contribution is going to matter more than God's contribution. The title for our talk this evening is, 'With Whose Resources?' And it turns out I think it's in my resources that the task of ministry will be done; that it's more important for me to be working than it is for me to be praying. Why is it that I find prayer so hard? Prayer ought to be easy. The hard work of prayer has been done by the Lord Jesus Christ on the cross two thousand years ago, and now the Father welcomes me into his presence through the blood of his Son. And, as if that wasn't enough, he gives me the Holy Spirit to help me pray, to pray with me, to interpret my groans and my longings. Prayer is easy; it is nothing more, nothing less, than a child asking their father for help. So why is it that I find it so hard?

Well, either I don't want that intimacy with my Father or I don't think I need his help. I think, actually, that what I do matters more than what he does; I think that my work is the important thing. I want to correct that thinking for us this evening as we look at some of the ways the Holy Spirit is at work in the lives and mission of his people in the book of Acts. I want to see what the Holy Spirit is doing in and through the mission of the church. I hope that will excite you but also that it will be a great encouragement to prayer.

So, turn first of all to the very opening of the book of Acts. In Acts 1:1–8 Jesus says, in effect, 'Don't do anything until you have received the power of the Holy Spirit.' But what I want you to notice is in verse 2 Luke talks about Jesus giving instructions through the Holy Spirit. Just think about that for a moment, Jesus giving instructions through the Holy Spirit. What does that mean? Does that mean that Jesus, the Son of God, the risen Lord, did his work through the Holy Spirit, needed the Holy Spirit to do his ministry? Apparently it does. He conducted his mission from beginning to end in the power of the Spirit. In fact, if you wind back to Luke's gospel – remember that Acts is the second half of the story that Luke began in his gospel – he talks about the Spirit coming on Jesus at his baptism, Jesus being led by the Spirit into the desert and then going into Galilee to begin his ministry of preaching in the power of the Holy Spirit. Jesus himself does his ministry in the power of the Spirit. The ministry Jesus does was done with the resources of God's Spirit and now he gives that Spirit to us. This is how we will do mission just as Jesus did: 'you will receive power when the Holy Spirit comes on you; and you will be my witnesses' (v.8). This is what happens on the day of Pentecost: the Holy Spirit comes on the people of God. And all the way through the book of Acts people receive the Holy Spirit when they become Christians and they are then empowered for mission. And I want to highlight five different ways, or five different things that the Spirit does through the people of God in the book of Acts.

The first is this: the Spirit directs the mission of God's people. At one point in the story of Acts, Acts 8:26, an angel tells Philip to go to the Gaza road – just that, go to the Gaza road – and when he gets there to wait by the road. And as you may remember, an Ethiopian official comes along and the Spirit says, 'Go and stand by the chariot.' When Philip does that he sees that the Ethiopian is reading from the Scriptures and he says to him, 'Do you understand what you are reading?' and the Ethiopian says, 'How can I, unless someone explains it to me?' So Philip gets into the chariot and explains the message of Jesus from the Old Testament. The Ethiopian is baptized and takes the gospel back to Ethiopia. Now, just imagine the Holy Spirit said to you, 'Go and have a cup of tea in one of the cafés in Keswick.' Then when you arrive the Spirit says, 'Go and sit on that particular table,' and you sit down. You notice on the table next to you somebody is reading the Bible and you say, 'Do you understand what you are reading?' And they say, 'How can I unless someone explains it to me?' Or imagine the Spirit said, 'Go and stand on the Penrith Road.' You go

and stand there and the Spirit says, 'Hitch a lift.' And you hitch a lift
and there is a Bible on the back seat and you say, 'Do you understand
this book that you are reading?' And they say, 'How can I, unless someone explains it to me?' Why does this never happen? Why does this
never happen to me? That is what I want to know. Perhaps it is
because I get up too soon from prayer each morning.

I visited Albania a couple of years ago and I was told that a young
man from the States felt the Spirit calling him to learn Albanian. This
was back in the eighties when Albania was a completely closed country, so this decision made no sense at all. But he went and lived near
the border of Albania and learnt Albanian. Then two or three years
later the borders opened up and he was able to go in immediately,
speaking fluent Albanian, and share the gospel with people. And many
of the churches that are now in Albania were started by people he first
had contact with as a result of the Holy Spirit's leading. I think sometimes we worry too much about strategy and planning. The Holy
Spirit is the great mission strategist; he is the one who directs the mission of God's people. He is, as it were, the one in the control room
moving the pieces around the board, organizing the mission of God's
people. It is the Holy Spirit who has the big picture, and I think there
is a great confidence and freedom in that. If you offer yourselves, if
you are open to the leading of God's Spirit, if you are faithful in what
is before you, then the Spirit will use that as part of the big picture he
sees. He is God's great mission strategist.

A little while later in the book of Acts a man called Cornelius, who
longs to know God, has a vision and is told to send people to Simon
Peter, one of the apostles. Meanwhile, Peter also has a vision and we
read in Acts 10, 'While Peter was still thinking about the vision, the
Spirit said to him, "Simon, three men are looking for you. So get up
and go downstairs. Do not hesitate to go with them, for I have sent
them"' (vv. 19–20). The Spirit tells Peter to go to these men, in a sense
a little bit like he told Philip to go to the Ethiopian. What I find so
striking is that not only does the Spirit bring Christians to unbelievers but the Spirit brings unbelievers to Christians. The Spirit says to
Peter in his vision, 'Do not hesitate to go with them, for I have sent
them' - I, the Holy Spirit, have sent them. The Spirit is working in the

lives of unbelievers, preparing them to hear the gospel and bringing them into contact with those who can tell them that gospel.

I remember hearing the story of a Christian couple in Iran. They were making a long journey and they agree that every day they will try and share the gospel with somebody on their journey. It is getting late; they come to a petrol station to refuel and there, standing outside the petrol station, is a man with a large beard and a rifle. The large beard is a sign he is a militant Muslim. And the wife says, 'I think you should tell him the gospel.' And the man says, 'You must be joking', and he refuses. So they fuel up and they are driving along the road but the wife won't let it go. She says, 'I just feel you should have told him the gospel. Why didn't you tell him the gospel?' She is going on at him and in the end the husband slams his foot on the brake and turns the car around and says, 'OK, if you want to be a widow I'll go and tell him the gospel!' He drives back to the petrol station. The man is still there. He goes up to the man and says, 'Do you want to know God?' And the man starts crying because three days before he had had a dream, and in that dream he had been told that if he wanted to know God he should go and stand at that particular spot, at that particular time. What I want to know is why does that never happen to me? Perhaps it is because I get up from prayer too soon each morning.

The Spirit directs the mission of God's people. Second, the Spirit gives faith when people hear God's Word. Peter goes with the men whom Cornelius has sent, and when he arrives Cornelius has gathered all his family and friends. So Peter suddenly finds himself with an audience and starts to proclaim the gospel. We read in Acts 10:44, 'While Peter was still speaking these words, the Holy Spirit came on all who heard the message. The circumcised believers who had come with Peter were astonished that the gift of the Holy Spirit had been poured out even on the Gentiles.'

A couple of months ago one of my wife's colleagues became a Christian. We got to know her and she loved hanging out with our gospel community, but she found the gospel message just weird. My wife and I did some Bible studies with her and it was really quite a lot of fun because we just suddenly saw the Bible afresh through the eyes of an unbeliever. Her eyes were popping all the time, 'Somebody walked on water?! Somebody ascended on clouds into heaven?! That is wacky, you know?' She gave her testimony a while ago and said, 'It was just so weird, but you all seemed like normal people and you were all holding down jobs!' Then she said she was sitting on her living room floor one evening and just in a moment she knew that it was true. What happened? Well I think the Holy Spirit came on her just as he did on Cornelius and his family. The Holy Spirit gave her faith in the Lord Jesus Christ and it was just wonderful to hear her tell her story. But why doesn't it happen more often? Perhaps it is because I get up from prayer too soon each morning.

Thirdly, the Spirit empowers God's people to speak God's Word. A couple of nights ago we were looking at the story of Peter and John healing a lame man at the temple. The man gets up, walks, and leaps around. A crowd gathers and as Peter is preaching to them the temple guard arrest them. The next day they are brought before the religious leaders and we are told in Acts 4:8, 'Peter, filled with the Holy Spirit, said to them . . .' And verse 13: 'When they [leaders of the Sanhedrin] saw the courage of Peter and John and realized they were unschooled, ordinary men, they were astonished and they took note that these men had been with Jesus.' They are astonished at his courage, he was just an ordinary guy with no education and people are astonished; that is what the Holy Spirit does. And maybe that is how you feel: you just feel like an ordinary kind of guy, no education, no fancy degrees, no theological training but through the Holy Spirit you can be empowered to speak God's words.

The religious leaders threaten Peter and John, telling them not to speak in the name of Jesus, and release them. Peter and John go back to the disciples and they pray together (Acts 4:23–31). This is the first time in the story of Acts and in the story of the church that the church has been threatened, and what do they pray? It is very interesting, isn't it? They don't pray for an end to persecution – in fact, they affirm that opposition is part of God's plan. They quote from Psalm 2. The nations have always opposed the Messiah; now they oppose his people. Instead, they pray for boldness and miracles. Acts 4:29 and 30: 'consider their threats and enable your servants to speak your word with great bold-ness. Stretch out your hand to heal and   perform miraculous signs and wonders'. Why that combination? I think the answer is that last time God performed a miracle two people got thrown into prison. I think it's as if they are saying, 'Lord, if you are going to perform these miraculous signs and heal people then you had better give us some boldness because we are going to get into trouble. And what happens? Acts 4:31: 'After they prayed, the place where they were meeting was shaken. And they were all filled with the Holy Spirit and spoke the word of God boldly.' What happens when you pray for boldness? God fills you with his Spirit. And what happens when God fills you with his Spirit? You proclaim the Word of God with boldness. Why don't I proclaim the word of God with boldness? Perhaps it's because I get up from prayer too soon each morning.

Fourthly, the Spirit confounds opposition to God's Word. Later in the story Paul and Barnabas come to Paphos (Acts 13:6). They get the opportunity to preach to the governor but a sorcerer called Elymas opposed them and tried to turn the proconsul from the faith. Paul, filled with the Holy Spirit, looked straight at Elymas and said, 'You are a child of the devil and an enemy of everything that is right! . . . Now the hand of the Lord is against you. You are going to be blind' (v. 10–11). Then, 'Immediately mist and darkness came over him,' and he had to be led away. The gospel is being preached, the sorcerer is trying to disrupt what is happening and Paul is filled with the Spirit and the opposition is confounded.

In Acts 6 we're told of the story of Stephen. He too performed miraculous signs and the members of the synagogue opposed him and argued with him, 'but they could not stand up against his wisdom or the Spirit by whom he spoke' (Acts 6:10). It's a very striking phrase, isn't it? And again, imagine when your friends laugh at you in the playground, or when the bloke in the office argues with you, or when people belittle your faith, or when they pick holes in what you say, imagine the Spirit speaking through you in a way that no one can refute. Imagine people saying they could not stand up against your wisdom or the power by which you spoke. Why am I unable to do that? Why am I unable to confound those who reject and ridicule God's Word? Perhaps it is because I get up from prayer too soon each morning.

Then, finally, the Spirit gives comfort and joy to God's people. Stephen, as he's speaking, is brought before the religious council. He bravely proclaims the gospel and they respond with fury – they are gnashing their teeth; they are in a kind of frenzy. And we read, 'Stephen, full of the Holy Spirit, looked up to heaven and saw the glory of God, and Jesus standing at the right hand of God' (Acts 7:55). Again, what a moment that is. God doesn't rescue Stephen. He dies a martyr, the first martyr – I think because God gets so much glory from the faithful suffering of his people. But in God's kindness the Holy Spirit gives Stephen a vision of the glory that is waiting for him. Soon after in Acts, Luke says the church throughout Judea, Galilee, Samaria enjoyed a time of peace; it was strengthened and encouraged by the Holy Spirit. Or, again, in Acts 13:52, the disciples 'were filled with joy and with the Holy Spirit'. Why am I not filled with joy in that way? Some of you, I suspect, struggle to find joy. Maybe you struggle to find joy in the pressures of motherhood, in your work situation, or because of your ailments or frailties. And our hearts do not rise above our circumstances to stand with Jesus in the presence of the Father. Why is it that people in your church struggle to find joy? Why is it that people in my church struggle to find joy? Perhaps it is because I get up from prayer too soon each morning.

As I was preparing, as I looked at what the Holy Spirit is doing throughout the story of Acts, I was struck by God's kindness: his kindness to the Ethiopian and Cornelius, sending someone to tell them about Jesus; his kindness to Stephen, opening heaven to him as he suffers; his kindness to the church, directing them in mission, guiding them, making them bold, giving them joy. And God has not stopped being kind, but maybe we have stopped praying. Why does God need our prayers to do his work? The answer, of course, is that he doesn't. He doesn't need our prayers, but it seems that he chooses to work through our prayers and I wonder if that is so, that we never presume that it's our work that matters most. If we worked without ever needing to pray then I suspect we would assume that it was our work that made the difference. So we have to pray so that we are constantly reminded that it is God's work and God's glory. It might be that we don't see more of God's blessing in our country because we don't pray.

Now, listen, I'm not worried about how long you pray. God doesn't time our prayers. In fact, in the Sermon on the Mount, Jesus is quite critical of long prayers, particularly if you are measuring them to prove their worth. God doesn't measure the worth of our prayers with a stopwatch. He measures the worth of our prayers by the blood of his precious Son. So I don't care whether you get up early to pray or you stay up late to pray but I do want us to pray as if God's work matters most, not our work.

See, that's my problem in the morning: I think my work is more important than God's work, that my contribution counts more than God's. Now, God could reach the world without us but he chooses to use us so what we do does matter. Our actions matter, our words matter, our witness matters; I don't want to deny that. But the problem is, instead of this being God's mission that he invites us to participate in, we think it's our mission and God can help if he wants. And so I don't pray, not really.

James says, 'The prayer of a righteous man is powerful and effective. Elijah was a man just like us. He prayed earnestly that it would not rain, and it did not rain in the land for three and a half years. Again he prayed and the heavens gave rain, and the earth produced its crops' (Jas 5:16–18). That phrase, 'he prayed earnestly', is literally, 'he prayed in his prayers'. That's quite striking, isn't it? He prayed in his prayers. Do you realize what that means? It means it's possible to pray without praying, to go through a duty, a ritual, a formality without really praying. We need to pray in our prayers, we need to pour ourselves into our prayers, pray fervently and earnestly as if our work depended on God and not on us. James says Elijah was just like us. He wasn't some kind of spiritual superhero. In fact Elijah may have prayed in his prayers but he also despaired in his despair. Elijah did depression in a serious way. He was just like us, but what marked him out was, he prayed in his prayers.

The Puritans used to talk about 'praying until you pray'. There is something good about duty; at its best it's faith saying, 'I don't feel like praying but I'm going to do it anyway until I do feel like it, until I really am praying and engaging with God, until I pray in my prayers.' So I'm not worried about how long you pray, but I want you to pray until you pray, to give yourself to prayer, to pour yourself into your prayers, to pray as if it's God's work that matters not your work. Remember prayer is nothing more, nothing less, than a child asking their father for help. Why don't I pray more? Because I don't think I need any help.

Let me end with a prayer. It's the words of Isaiah in chapter 64:6–9: 'All of us have become like one who is unclean, and all our righteous acts are like filthy rags; we all shrivel up like a leaf, and like the wind our sins sweep us away. No one calls on your name or strives to lay hold of you; for you have hidden your face from us and made us waste away because of our sins. Yet, O LORD, you are our Father. We are the clay, you are the potter; we are all the work of your hand. Do not be angry beyond measure, O LORD; do not remember our sins for ever. Oh, look upon us we pray, for we are all your people.' Amen.

Mission by whom?

By Steve Brady

Steve Brady

Steve Brady was born in Liverpool where he was converted in his teens. He is married with two children and three grandchildren and has been in full-time Christian ministry for over thirty years. He is Principal of Moorlands College and the author of the Keswick Study Guides on Colossians and Galatians. A keen sportsman and author, he hates gardening and still has an irrational attachment to Everton Football Club!

Mission by whom? Isaiah 6

About a century ago the Antarctic explorer Sir Ernest Shackleton put an advert in the daily newspapers, 'Men wanted for hazardous journey – small wages, bitter cold, long months of complete darkness, constant danger, safe return doubtful.' And hundreds and hundreds of guys applied to go with him, obviously one or two having marriage problems! When it comes to world mission – 'Mission by whom?' – what kind of people is it God wants to send? Tough, resilient, SAS types, folk who have got it altogether? Or those who everyone knows to be utter wimps?

What kind of people does God want to send on his mission? Major Ian Thomas used to talk about God always looking for a bush like the burning bush. And when it comes to the bush, any bush will do as long as it's prepared to burn for God. Because there are no great gifts and no great talents that God wants to use, only people whose hearts and lives are surrendered to him so that through us, in all our weakness, inadequacy and insufficiency, God may get his work done in his world.

As we turn to Isaiah 6, we hear the great call from the Almighty, 'Whom shall I send? And who will go for us?' (v.8). I want to suggest from this passage a number of things about the people who are to go. 'Whom shall I send?' Who is God going to send? Firstly, it's those who glimpse the glory of God.

Isaiah talks about it at the beginning of the chapter: 'In the year that King Uzziah died.' King Uzziah had been a comparatively good King.

He didn't finish well but he started well and he reigned for over fifty years. And here we are now in 740 BC and a major prop has been knocked out of the life of a nation. Maybe since the last Keswick some major prop has been knocked out of your life. I was speaking to a friend at lunchtime and her husband, just in his mid-sixties, has been taken ill in these last twelve months or so. Maybe in your own personal circumstances you can immediately identify someone or something that has been taken from you. Maybe your job, your health or whatever, and now things are different from what they used to be. And here in this pivotal period in the life of a nation, this great King who has reigned for decades and decades is gone.

Of course, there is something about Uzziah you need to know. It is recorded in 2 Chronicles 26:16: 'after Uzziah became powerful, his pride led to his downfall.' He intruded into the office of the priest, which was strictly forbidden, and the result was that he was struck down by some incurable skin disease. It's often called leprosy but we don't know what it was. It alienated him from his people and his community. He could no longer go up to the temple and he finished his life that had started with a bang with a whimper. That's salutary, isn't it? The great George Müller used to pray, 'Lord, save me from becoming a wicked old man.' Now there are a few old codgers here tonight, aren't there? I know – I am one of them! And I need to pray, 'Lord, save me from becoming a wicked old man.' Like they used to say in those financial adverts, 'Past performance is no guarantee of future success.' In other words, you can start off well but you may not finish well. This King Uzziah started well but finished badly.

But in the year that Uzziah died Isaiah says, 'I saw the LORD, seated on a throne'. Now, hang on a moment, Isaiah, you can't see God! Exodus 33 says, 'no one may see me and live' (v. 20). And if we could fast forward, Isaiah, you'll know that John writes, 'No one has ever seen God' (John 1:18). So, Isaiah, you need a reality check; you need to come to Moorlands Christian College so we can sort your theology out for you! Don't you know, Isaiah, that God is immortal and invisible, God only wise? O, yes, he knows that, but God throughout the Old Testament clothed himself, as it were, here and there, physically appearing, revealing aspects of his being and nature. Of course, this is pointing forward to that day when the Word who was God would literally become flesh and dwell amongst us.

In the year that the great king dies Isaiah catches a glimpse of the deathless King, the eternal Lord, the everlasting God, the immortal sovereign. Notice he is on a throne, reminding us of his authority. He rules amongst the armies of heaven and amongst the inhabitants of men. 'No one can hold back his hand or say to him: "What have you done?"' (Daniel 4:35). God is still on the throne. He reigns on high, he is majestic, he cannot be contained, he's immense and he's glorious. These burning ones before this glorious, eternal God, veil their faces and cry out to one another, 'Holy, holy, holy is the Lord Almighty; the whole earth is full of his glory' (Isa. 6:3). Why do they say that? This is a unique expression in the Old Testament. When you want to make something a superlative in Hebrew you repeat it, so the 'Song of Songs' is the best of songs, the 'gold of gold' means the best gold. Now here we have this unique expression – it's not just the holy of holies; this is a superlative of a superlative – the holiest of the holiest. This word 'holy' has the idea of brightness, and the seraphs are bright, burning characters. But 'holy' also means to make a distinction, a difference, to be separate from. Isaiah is encountering the transcendence of God. The what? He is encountering the fact that the God before whom he stands is immeasurable, incomprehensible. He is eternal, the great I AM, who was and is and is to come.

You know, much of our evangelical worship is incredibly banal. It's trivial, it's like we have lost God somewhere. Thank God we are seeing some really good new songs coming through. But, you know, there have been periods in evangelicalism these last twenty-five or thirty years when it's no longer God Almighty; it's God all-matey. Does that ring any bells? The otherness, the transcendent glory of God, what the Puritans used to call his 'aseity', his endless being, his immensity, that is what Isaiah glimpses. Too much of our stuff is on the horizontal. Why is this important, by the way? You say, 'I don't want to listen to all the stuff about how great God is. You don't know how many problems I've got.' That's your problem! My favourite verse is Hebrews 12:2: 'looking unto Jesus, the author and finisher of our faith' (NKJV) – not looking to myself, not looking to my problems. If

I take the living God here in my left hand and this book, here is all my problems, stick them between myself and the Lord and you know what I begin to sing? 'Nobody knows the trouble I've seen!' But what do you think happens when the living God comes between yourself and your problems? It's not that they disappear, but that suddenly you are lost in wonder, love and praise. That's what real Christian worship is meant to do for us. We used to sing, 'Let's forget about ourselves and concentrate on him and worship him.' We are all worshipping beings; we can't help it. And what the gospel does is re-orientate us. Do you not realize that this God is glorious in all the earth?

And, by the way, it would be massively irresponsible of me not to remind you that this vision Isaiah sees is quoted by John: 'Isaiah said this because he saw Jesus' glory and spoke about him' (John 12:41). Wow! Old Testament saints tried to work out the full revelation of the one God promised to come and visit us in the person we know as Jesus, the eternal Son of God. The glory of God, says 2 Corinthians 4, was seen in the face of Christ, who is the image of God (see vv. 4, 6). The glory of God was made manifest through the one we call our Lord Jesus Christ. What has this got to do with mission? In a word, everything.

William C. Burns was a contemporary and friend of the saintly Robert Murray McCheyne. In his early thirties he was called to go to China. When he was learning the Chinese language and about to set sail somebody rather sarcastically said to him, 'I suppose you are going to China to save a few Chinese?' He replied, 'No, I'm going there for the glory of God.' There are other motives for mission but most of all it's about the glory of God. Stanley Baldwin was a British Prime Minister on three occasions. He was someone misunderstood; at least, his son A.M. Baldwin thought so. So when his father died his son, A.M. Baldwin, wrote a book, *My Father – the True Story*. Why do we get involved in mission? Because people out there believe all sorts of other stories about the living God. A sophisticated person who would never worship a metal image but says, 'I would like to think of God like this . . .' has an idolatrous mental image. And the gospel is telling the story about how you need to throw away all your false gods and find this one true Father and his true story as narrated by his Son.

'Whom shall I send?' Not only do we need people who have glimpsed the glory of God but, secondly, we need those who recognize the reality of sin. Last century, a man called Rudolph Otto, a philosopher, wrote a book called *The Idea of the Holy*. In the book he used the word 'numinous' to explain our 'creatureliness' and our creature-consciousness before the inexplicable. On one level it might be when you get a sense of the creeps, something is eerie; it may be 'ghosts'. At the other end of the spectrum it might be when you get a sense of your smallness before the ineffable majesty of God.

Is that what is happening here? As he stands before the magnificence of God he feels very small. Is that what is being expressed here? No, this is not smallness before the immensity of God; this is sinfulness before the purity of God. That's why he cries out as he catches this glimpse of this holy God, 'Woe to me! . . . I am ruined!' (Isa. 6:5). I am torn apart as I stand before this holy God who knows everything I've ever thought, said and done. I stand in need of mercy. And he says not only that – 'I am ruined! For I am a man of unclean lips, and I live among a people of unclean lips'. If you go through those early chapters of Isaiah you will come across some shocking things. Chapter 2:6: 'They are full of superstitions from the East'. Well, thank goodness we don't have superstition in Britain today, do we? Touch wood! Chapter 3:4: 'I will make boys their officials; mere children will govern them.' Amateurs in politics - well, we don't have that either, do we? In Chapter 3:16 the Lord said, 'The women of Zion are haughty, walking along with outstretched necks, flirting with their eyes, tripping along with mincing steps'. We don't have anything like that in our culture, do we? Catwalks and 'Colour Me Beautiful' – some of us need all the help we can get, I suppose! By chapter 5:20 you've got moral chaos: 'Woe to those who call evil good and good evil'. Now, we don't have anything like that in Great Britain, do we?

Hello! Aren't we living in a topsy-turvy, morally chaotic period in our world where Christians have to apologize for being Christians and believing in right and wrong and everything is a thousand and one shades of grey? Isaiah's physical disease became a metaphor for the whole nation of Judah, 'Why should you be beaten any more? . . . Your whole head is injured, your whole heart afflicted. From the sole of your foot to the top of your head there is no soundness – only wounds and bruises and open sores, not cleansed or bandaged or soothed with oil' (Isa. 1:5,6). Isaiah is here before the Lord and he knows he is part of a sinful race. He knows himself to be sinful before a holy God. You are never qualified to go and serve the Lord until you know that you have got a sinful heart and, but for the restraining grace of God, there is nothing you are not capable of.

One of the hard tasks we sometimes have with our students at Moorlands is helping them to recognize their arrogance and pride and realize that they are not God's gift. Unless they get to know themselves and the weakness of their own hearts, they are going to be a liability in Christian ministry. God sends broken people redeemed by his grace to tell other broken people where they can be put together again.

'Whom shall I send?' Who does God send into mission? People who glimpse the glory of God, people who recognize the reality of sin and, thirdly, people who know the certainty of forgiveness. Why did the seraphs fly with a live coal from off the altar? It's the altar of sacrifice. And what happened at this altar of sacrifice? They offered sacrifice for sin, blood sacrifices; it was the place of atonement, a place where you found forgiveness. That's why there is that interesting phrase in verse 7, 'With it he touched my mouth and said, "See."' Older translations say, 'Behold', and that's a big biblical word. In the New Testament it is used similarly when John the Baptist sees Jesus and says, 'Behold' – see, take note, stop, pay attention; you, at the back, are you listening? It's that kind of thing. 'Behold the Lamb of God who takes away the sin of the world' (John 1:29). We are not imposing stuff on the biblical record here. Isaiah the prophet is looking forward.

Sigmund Freud did the world a great disservice when he drove a wedge between sin and guilt. Of course, you can have false guilt but people rightly feel guilty when they break the laws of God. They may expunge that guilt in drugs, sex, rock and roll, alcohol and a dozen other things. But Isaiah knows that before this God he is guilty. Do you? And that's why the cross is essential – it is God's only remedy for sin. It is not a case of 'cosmic child abuse', an innocent victim suffering for something he didn't do wrong; that is to completely misunderstand the cross.

Jesus Christ is not some third party. There is not this angry God and this nice Jesus. It's not that Jesus saw how wicked man had been and knew God must punish sin so out of pity he said he would bear the punishment; that's not biblical. It's God who so loved the world that he gave his Son.

The great missionary Hudson Taylor, as a young medic, read a little tract called *The Finished Work of Christ*, and through it he found peace with God. He said, 'I saw the whole work was done, the whole debt was paid and there was nothing more for me to do than to accept what he offered and praise him evermore.' That's an interesting phrase at the end: when he saw the wondrous cross he wanted to praise God evermore.

That leads to our fourth thing. The people God sends on his mission sense the enormity of the task. I have the privilege of speaking fairly regularly at ministers' inductions and ordinations. I can't ever remember anybody wanting to read this verse: 'Whom shall I send? And who will go for us?' . . . 'Here am I. Send me!' (v.8). It would have been good to stop the reading there, wouldn't it? Just look at the rest of Isaiah. God seems to be saying to Isaiah, 'Make the heart of these people calloused otherwise they may see with their eyes, hear with their ears, understand with their hearts and turn and be healed. Your ministry, Isaiah, is going to be fantastic, it's going to be a complete failure. Get over yourself.' There are times when God calls us to hard and seemingly fruitless ministries, where we feel people's hearts are so hard and yet, out of gratitude for Jesus, out of thankfulness for all God has done for us, we press on. At one level, wherever we go it is hard for the gospel. We would have to be really stupid not to realize it is getting more difficult in the British Isles today. A strong and often militant form of Islam on the one side and the siren sounds of secular atheism on the other. Some of us may be called tonight to some hard and seemingly unremitting commissions to serve the King. And we keep going, week in, week out, year in, year out, in sheer dogged determination and obedience with gratitude in our hearts, knowing that our labour in the Lord will not be in vain.

'Whom shall I send?' People who glimpse the glory of God. 'Whom shall I send?' Those who recognize the reality of sin, both their own and others. 'Whom shall I send?' People who know the certainty of forgiveness. 'Whom shall I send?' People who sense the enormity of the situation – unless God turns up we've had it! And finally, 'Whom shall I send?' People who believe in the importance of the mission.

Isaiah 6:13: 'But as the terebinth and oak leave stumps when they are cut down, so the holy seed will be the stump in the land.' Over in chapter 11:1: 'A shoot will come up from the stump of Jesse; from his roots a Branch will bear fruit.' By verse 10 we are told, 'the Root of Jesse will stand as a banner for the peoples,' and if we are still scratching our heads by the time we get to Isaiah 53:2, this same theme is coming through – he was 'like a root out of dry ground.' And yet this root out of dry ground, this stump from nowhere: 'After the suffering of his soul, he will see the light of life and be satisfied; by his knowledge my righteous servant will justify many, and he will bear their iniquities' (Isa. 53:11). That idea of root and stump and then seed runs right through Scripture from Genesis 3 – the seed of the woman will bruise the serpent's head – to Galatians 3 where we are told that the seed is Christ. So the whole Bible hangs together round mission but it primarily hangs together round the Lord Jesus himself. And as Isaiah catches this glimpse of the glory and magnificence and otherness of God he's given this terrible commission and told the holy seed will be the stump in the land. Where is it all going to end, Isaiah? In abject failure, the church eclipsed, everything shutting down.

In 1749 Bishop Butler, when he was offered the see of Canterbury, said, 'It is too late to support a falling church.' He turned down being Archbishop because he thought, in the words of that great Scottish saint from *Dad's Army*, 'We're all doomed, Captain Mainwaring, we're all doomed.' In the early eighteenth century, between 1695 and 1730, only one new non-conformist church was built in the whole of London. The great men of the Church of England said that non-conformity would die out in a generation and Christianity, maybe, a generation after that. But hymn writer and Pastor Isaac Watts didn't just take his cue from the signs of doom and gloom for Christianity in the early eighteenth century. He read his Bible, he believed what God said in Psalm 72, he will reign forever 'from the River to the ends of the earth.' And long before the Methodists were in the great revival, thirteen years before William Carey, the father of modern missions, was born, Isaac Watts sat down and wrote a hymn. It was a statement of faith – you may have heard of it – 'Jesus shall reign where'er the sun, doth his successive journeys run, his kingdom stretch from shore to shore, till moons shall wax and wane no more.' And around the world today Jesus Christ is building his church; we have so much encouragement if only we would lift up our eyes to see. A man like Watts knew that the best days of the church were going to be ahead.

Here is Isaiah, 740 years before the birth of Christ, looking down through the centuries. And he is given a promise that God's kingdom and God's purposes will not fail, so the question comes, 'Whom shall I send?' And you notice what Isaiah says, 'Take my wife and let me be. I consecrate her Lord to thee, take her moments and her days, and mine shall flow in ceaseless praise.' Is that what it says? Or does it say, 'God, I know you're really hard pushed; it must be tough running the whole universe, you need me. God, you are a Trinity but if I joined you we could become a "quadrinity". We could make things really hum round here. God I think you need me.' The Lord doesn't need anybody. He's self-sufficient yet in his amazing grace the call comes tonight, 'Whom shall I send?' Whom shall I send to that sink housing estate, back to that difficult home, to that tough church where they don't even have Bibles, never mind let you preach from them? Whom shall I send to that dreadful factory where you are laughed at, to that Islamic world which so needs to come to know the wonderful submission and freedom that comes from belonging to Jesus, to the Hindu world with their multiplicity of gods, the Buddhist world, the secular world, the scientific world, the political world, the academic world, the world of theology? Whom shall I send? And who will go for us? Isaiah doesn't say, 'Well, I suppose you had better send me.' No, no. Do you remember those days when the teacher wanted a little job done and you could get out of class for five minutes – 'I want a volunteer?' Everyone's a volunteer. 'Yes, Miss, me, me, ME!' It's that kind of picture! 'Whom shall I send?' 'O Lord, please send me'. And God did, and the world has never been the same. And God may send you – what a privilege – and your world and maybe generations unborn will never be the same.

For how long?

By Derek Burnside

Derek Burnside

Derek Burnside is a Trustee of Keswick Ministries and is on the staff and leadership team at Belmont Chapel in Exeter. He is married to Penny, a primary school head teacher, and teaches at four of the Torchbearer's European Bible schools as well as being on the councils of the Evangelical Alliance and Partnership UK, the network of British churches from Brethren backgrounds. Before any of that he taught RE in a large comprehensive school and was a UCCF staff worker.

For how long? 1 Timothy 6:11–16

Tonight's question is, 'Mission – for how long?' 'How long?' is an important question. Knowing how long something is going to last generally helps us live better in the moment. Some of us will be going home tomorrow and will be thinking, 'How long is the journey? It's 200 miles. I'll have to stop at the petrol station on Penrith Road.' Some of you may be heading out to the hills tomorrow morning, 'How long is the walk? Twenty miles. I am going to need four litres of water, two rounds of sandwiches, a couple of mars bars, two apples and the number of the mountain rescue team!' Some of you might go home tomorrow night and wonder about going to the movies. 'How long is the film? Two and a half hours. Well, let's go to the toilet right now!'

But sometimes we just don't know exactly how long something is going to last. And often that is true for some of the most important things in life. We know there is going to be an end point but we don't know exactly when. And we have to learn to live life in the light of the unspecified end point. 'How long until my unsaved children and grand-children come to the Lord?' Well, apart from the Lord, nobody really knows. 'How long until God heals me?' Well, apart from the Lord, nobody knows. 'How long am I going to live for?' Well, nobody really knows. 'How long is this guy going to be speaking for tonight?' Nobody really knows. And this one is especially for those who are still in paid employment: 'How long until I retire?' Well, nobody really knows.

The most important things in life often have an end point but we don't know exactly when that is going to be – we need to learn to live in the light of an unspecified end. It is a vital life skill. Our question tonight is, 'Mission, for how long?' How long are we on mission for? When can we stop fighting the good fight of the faith? When can we stop running the race? We have a clear command and this is our first idea tonight. In 1 Timothy 6:13,14 Paul says, 'I charge you to keep this command without spot or blame' – and he is talking about the command to fight the good fight of faith and take hold of the eternal life that Timothy received when he made his good confession for Christ – 'until the appearing of our Lord Jesus Christ'. That is our answer tonight. 'How long are we on mission for?' We are on mission until the Lord Jesus Christ appears.

Do you think much about the appearing of Christ? Does that idea fill your head and your heart much? Do you remember *The Miracle Maker*, an animated version of Luke's gospel? When I was in the cinema watching this beautiful portrayal of Christ's life, albeit in animated clay, I found myself crying. I don't often cry in films but I just found myself weeping. I was trying to work out why I was crying and I think it was because *The Miracle Maker* was so well done I was getting a little flickering glimmer of Jesus Christ in flesh. I think I was getting a tiny little premonition of what it was going to be like to see him face to face, what it was going to be like when he appears. And I found myself just looking forward to that moment so much. Do you do that?

We are filled with the Spirit of the Lord Jesus Christ. He has promised never to leave us or forsake us. The Spirit brings his power and his presence into our lives. But one day Jesus will appear. It will either be when he comes again at his glorious second coming or when we die and are in paradise with him. He is going to appear to us. When will that be? How long to wait until he appears? Well we don't exactly know. What does Paul say? 'God will bring [it] about in his own time' (1 Tim. 6:15). Other than the Father, nobody really knows.

Tell me what you make of this: 'As one looks at the world today, as one takes up the Word of God and the daily newspaper, we are conscious that we are on the verge of great events. You remember some of the disciples got alone with the Master one day and said, "Lord, what shall be the sign of thy coming and of the end of the age?" And our Lord gave some signs and some indications. And we study those chapters concerning those signs and indications. As we see events happening in the church, in Palestine and among the Jews, events that are happening in the nations – mens' hearts failing them for fear, we are under the profound conviction that the coming of the Lord cannot be far off.' As we look at the world and pick up our Bibles and our newspapers, as we think about the chapters, the signs that Jesus gave for his second coming being imminent, our author says that we are under the profound conviction that the coming of the Lord cannot be far off.

Those words were spoken from the Keswick Convention tent, eighty years ago on Monday 13 July 1931. At the Convention of 1931 the Revd E.L. Langston preached an address called *The Great Examination Day*. And his growing conviction was that the return of the Lord Jesus would be soon. I suspect if we had said to the Revd Langston that night, in eighty years time the Convention would still be here, he would have been surprised and a little disappointed. We are on mission until the appearing of the Lord Jesus Christ. 'How long is that going to be?' We don't know. But we do know that for those of us in this tent Jesus has not yet appeared. So on this night, our charge, our instruction, our command, whoever we are, whatever our age or setting, is clear. We are still on mission – all of us in this tent. The charge to fight the good fight of the faith is our clear command.

Now, when it comes to Timothy, I am not sure that is the answer he was hoping for. We get several hints in Paul's first letter to Timothy that Paul is writing to a pretty weary warrior. This is our second idea tonight – a pretty weary warrior who is sorely tempted to give up. Just look for a minute at 2 Thessalonians 1:3 and see how Paul starts the letter. 'We ought always to thank God for you, brothers, and rightly so, because your faith is growing'. Flick back to 1 Thessalonians 1:2, 'We always thank God for all of you, mentioning you in our prayers.' Are you seeing a pattern emerge of how Paul starts his letters? Look at Colossians 1:3,4: 'We always thank God, the Father of our Lord Jesus Christ, when we pray for you, because we have heard of your faith in Christ Jesus and

of the love you have for all the saints'. Let's try Philippians 1:3,4: 'I
thank my God every time I remember you. In all my prayers for all of
you'. And Ephesians 1:15,16: 'For this reason, ever since I heard about
your faith in the Lord Jesus and your love for all the saints, I have not
stopped giving thanks for you, remembering you in my prayers.'

Do you notice the way Paul habitually starts his letters with thanksgiving? Flick back to 1 Timothy. Do you see the way he starts this
one? Verse 3: 'As I urged you when I went into Macedonia, stay there
in Ephesus'. This is an unusual start. Galatians is the only other letter
with this absence of thanksgiving. Paul's words are not thanksgiving
for Timothy's robust, fruit-bearing faith. His words come from a deep
concern that his son in the faith might be on the verge of just walking away from his mission. Timothy sounds like a weary warrior as we
read between the lines of 1 and 2 Timothy.

I think Timothy is close to burn-out when this letter arrives on his
desk. And we can understand why when we think about his setting.
Timothy is in a tough spot – Ephesus is not an easy city. We know
this from Luke's account in Acts 19 when he records the time Paul
spent in the city founding this church. Luke describes the Jews as
'obstinate; they refused to believe and publicly maligned the Way'
(v.9). And if Jewish opposition wasn't enough, when the gospel did
start to make some ground and people started to get saved, the Greeks
rioted and Paul had to leave the city. Ephesus is a tough place to do
ministry. There was obstinacy, a refusal to believe, publicly insulting the
faith or when ground is won, a full-blown riot. Does that ring any
bells in the settings you are going back to tonight or tomorrow?

Surely by now, by the time Paul writes 1 Timothy, things will have
changed? Presumably, five years on Timothy is leading a biblical, united,
passionate, prayerful, godly church who can stand together and make
inroads into this kind of community? No, he is not. The Ephesian church
– probably just a network of churches forming one congregation – was
a mess. Do you ever hear people say, 'I would love it if we could just get
back to being like the first-century church.' Really? You want churches
like that?

If you are a home group member in your church could you raise
your hand? Quite a few. If you are a home group leader keep your

hand up? Lots of them. I want you to imagine that I am giving you three new members in your home group. I'm going to give you James. He has a real 'bee in his bonnet' about the genealogies in the Bible. It is stuff that is not central to the gospel or to the mission of the church but he has turned a minor detail into a central tenant of doctrine. He has become obsessed by it; he can't stop talking about it. And you are starting to suspect that it is an avoidance strategy. He gets self-righteous and argumentative so he can actually avoid dealing with the main issue of proclaiming the gospel to lost people. And if it was just James it wouldn't be that bad, but there are younger members in your home group that are being influenced by it and a squabble has started to break out over this nonsense. It is 7:25 p.m. on a Wednesday night and the door bell is going to ring. James is about to arrive in your home group. How do you feel about that?

I am giving you another new member – Kenneth. He has issues around rather twisted forms of doctrine. He thinks that spiritual wholeness and well-being come through what you eat and drink. So for him alcohol is absolutely off limits and he says there are certain types of food you shouldn't touch. He has started saying that nobody should get married and if you are already married you certainly shouldn't be having sex. He has started measuring spiritual maturity by what you don't eat, what you don't drink and certainly what you don't get up to. It is 7:25 p.m. on Wednesday night and Kenneth is about to arrive at the door for home group.

Can I give you one more? Sarah. Sarah is a believer but you are convinced that she is in serious spiritual drift. Her love of money and the comfort and possessions it brings are becoming her first love. That means that Sarah and her family are making all sorts of decisions and choosing lots of odd priorities that seem to have less and less to do with the gospel. That is your home group. The doorbell rings and you go, 'Yes! Home group! Fantastic!'

If you had that sort of group would you not think, 'How much longer? How long am I on mission with these people? How much longer do I have to fight the fight of the faith with this group? How much longer are you asking me to pastor, teach, correct and encourage them? For how much longer am I to set an example and to spur them to love and good deeds? How much longer am I to lead them out to preach the gospel to an incredibly hostile world?' This is hard. And Timothy is trying to cope with all of those issues. Paul uses phrases like 'myths and endless genealogies' that were rife in the Corinthian church (1 Tim. 1:4). He talks about Timothy having to squash an unhealthy interest in controversies and quarrels. He talks about people's love of money which means they have wandered from the faith and pierced themselves with many griefs. He talks about people forbidding marriage and about commanding other church members to abstain from certain foods. And Timothy has to crush this false teaching while trying to do the work of an evangelist in a deeply hostile town and setting an example for the believers. Timothy is well and truly on mission in Ephesus. He is probably about 35 years old but he is weary and frequently ill. It sounds like he is intimidated by some of the older members of the church, he is timid, and he may even be tempted to cave into the lies that these false teachers are propagating.

It would be very unusual in a crowd of this number tonight if we don't have some pretty weary warriors. If you are at the end of Week 2 of the Keswick Convention, it has been our intense and sincere prayer that those who came spiritually or physically weary have been revitalized and re-energized by the Spirit of God, by the preaching of his Word, by the fellowship with his people, and by the beauty of his creation.

In his lovely little book, *The Roots of Endurance*, John Piper compares what he calls 'coronary Christians' to 'adrenal Christians'. By coronary he means to do with the heart and by adrenal he means to do with adrenaline. He says that adrenaline only keeps us going for short spurts, it gets you through Sunday but you're tired by Monday. Whereas the heart keeps going steadily, consistently, on good days and bad.

I want to be a coronary Christian – don't you? A passionate Christian with the heart beat of the Lord Jesus Christ. I want to be in a community of Christians like that – steady, enduring, passionate - not adrenal Christians known for their fits and starts. I want to fight the good fight of the faith without spot or blame until he appears. I want to keep on mission until he comes. And I suspect tonight we have a tent full of believers who want just the same thing, who want what Paul wanted for Timothy. And in 1 Timothy 6:11,12 Paul gives Timothy a very simple strategy for coronary Christianity and, as we close, we are going to look at these three simple steps.

Firstly, 'flee'. Chapter 6:11: 'flee from all this.' Paul doesn't mean flee Ephesus; he says right at the start of the letter, 'I urge you to stay' (see 1 Tim. 1:3). Don't flee the mission, don't run away from the charge or the commission you have been given. Paul says flee from the rubbish in Ephesus. He's talking about the false teaching, the stupid arguments, the conceited love of self that marks so many false teachers, the quarrels, the friction and the love of money. Just flee from all that rubbish. Paul says to Timothy, 'Run! Flee! Flee from this junk.' And tonight if we have put anything in the middle of our theology or our lives that shouldn't be there – flee! If you are in the process of nudging Jesus Christ off the throne of your life and replacing him with money – flee.

Have you heard what is happening in some areas where rich divorcing couples are trying to work out which one gets the dog? Apparently they take the dog to the kennels for a month and neither partner gets to see the dog. And then after a month they go into the lawyer's office and one member of the couple sits at one end of the table and the other sits at the other end and somebody from the kennels brings the dog in. And both of them go, 'Come on boy, come on!' And the one which the dog goes to first gets to keep the dog. Let's imagine we are the dog and we are walking into a room, and at one end of the table sits Jesus and at the other end sits money and both of them call to us – which one do we run to? Jesus – wonderful! If there is anybody in this tent who is thinking, 'You know what, at the moment, if I am honest, I am not sure.' 'Flee,' Paul says, 'flee'.

The second step in this simple strategy is, 'fly'. The image in these verses is of running away from the bad stuff and running towards Christ. *Flee from and fly towards.* Verse 12 says, 'Take hold of the eternal life to which you were called when you made your good confession'. When Timothy became a Christian Paul says he ran into the arms of the one who promised life in all its fullness. He ran into the arms of the Lord Jesus Christ. So Paul tells Timothy, 'Fly to Jesus. Run to him, embrace him, and hold him. Take hold of that eternal life, that abundant life that you already have in Jesus. Cling to him, hold fast to him – hold tight.' And do you see those lovely words in verse 11? Cling to his righteousness and his godliness and his faith and his love and his endurance and his gentleness. This is Christ's heart, this is the heart we were given. This is the spirit we have been given. Not 'a spirit of timidity, but a spirit of power, of love and of self-discipline' (2 Tim. 1:7). So flee from the rubbish and fly to Christ and to the eternal life you have in him.

The third step in this simple strategy is fight. Just fight. 'Fight the good fight of the faith' (1 Tim. 6:12). We are going to fight with righteousness, with godliness and with faith. We are going to fight with love and gentleness. It is a strange kind of fighting, isn't it? But it is a fight. On Tuesday evening Bishop Michael Nazir-Ali was reflecting on the international reputation and heritage the Keswick Convention has. He said something like this: 'This is Keswick's legacy – an insistence on sacrificial service in the cause of the gospel, a renewal of passion for snatching from the flames all we can.' That is a fight, isn't it? This is Keswick's legacy – an insistence on sacrificial service in the cause of the gospel.

If you want to watch a really great movie can I recommend one called *The Guardian*. If you know the movie *Top Gun*, it is like that but with navy coastguard rescue swimmers. There is a great scene when the rookie navy coastguard swimmers – these are people who jump out of helicopters into water to save drowning people – are at the start of their training and the training officer says to them, 'If by some miracle you actually have what it takes to become one of us then you get to live a life of meagre pay, with the distinct possibility of dying slow, cold and alone somewhere in the sea. However you also get the chance to save lives and there is no greater calling in the world than that.'[1] So ladies and gentlemen – welcome to the greatest calling in the world. You get to save lives. There is no greater calling in the world than to fight the good fight until the Lord appears.

---

[1]   *The Guardian* © 2006 Touchstone.

John Stott's final book was *The Radical Disciple* and if you have read it you know he identifies several distinctive characteristics of a disciple. The final chapter is entitled, 'Death – the mark of a true disciple who is going to die to self and live to Christ'. And in that final chapter John Stott reminds us not to underestimate the cost of dying to self and living for Christ. He says we must die to ambition, we must put aside our desire for security in the face of persecution and martyrdom, and we must die to this world as we prepare for our final destiny. Sounds like a fight to me.

It has been such a privilege to spend this week in the company of brothers and sisters who take that call seriously. It is eighty years and sixteen days since E.L. Langston preached at Keswick and he may have been mistaken when he said that the Lord's coming was imminent in 1931, but he certainly got this right, and I am going to finish with his words: 'There lies upon every soul in this tent a solemn obligation we are to be in this world what the Saviour was. "As my Father has sent me even so I send you." His love was a Calvary love – a sacrificial love. His life was a sacrificial life, ever doing the will of the Father. In the light of the issues of life and the responsibilities of today and tomorrow, knowing as we do that God has brought us here to face these things, what is to be our response? Shall we not say, "Lord, reveal to me the things that are wrong? Show me the hidden things. Bring me to that place where I can be the best for thee. That nothing but gold and silver and precious stones will be put into that building so that in that day I may not be ashamed before thee at thy appearing."'[2]

---

[2] E.L. Langston, 'The Great Examination', in *Keswick Year Book 1931* (published 'by authority of the council'), page 105.

Keswick 2011

Keswick Convention 2011 teaching is available now
All Bible readings and talks recorded at Keswick 2011, including
Ajith Fernando, Chris Wright, Peter Maiden, Steve Brady, Helen
Roseveare, Michael Nazir-Ali and Richard Tiplady are available now
on CD, DVD★, MP3 download and USB stick from
www.essentialchristian.com/keswick

Keswick teaching now available on MP3 download
Just select the MP3 option on the teaching you want, and after
paying at the checkout your computer will receive the teaching
MP3 download – now you can listen to teaching on the go;
on your iPod, MP3 player or even your mobile phone.

Over fifty years of Keswick teaching all in one place
Visit www.essentialchristian.com/keswick to browse Keswick
Convention Bible teaching as far back as 1957! You can also browse
albums by worship leaders and artistes who performed at Keswick,
including Stuart Townend, Phatfish and Keith & Kristyn Getty, plus
Keswick Live albums and the *Precious Moments* collection of DVDs.

To order, visit www.essentialchristian.com/keswick or
call 0845 607 1672

★Not all talks available on DVD.

KESWICK MINISTRIES

Keswick Ministries is committed to the deepening of the spiritual life in individuals and church communities through the careful exposition and application of Scripture, seeking to encourage the following:

Lordship of Christ – To encourage submission to the Lordship of Christ in personal and corporate living

Life Transformation – To encourage a dependency upon the indwelling and fullness of the Holy Spirit for life transformation and effective living

Evangelism and Mission – To provoke a strong commitment to the breadth of evangelism and mission in the British Isles and worldwide

Discipleship – To stimulate the discipling and training of people of all ages in godliness, service and sacrificial living

Unity – To provide a practical demonstration of evangelical unity

Keswick Ministries is committed to achieving its aims by:

● providing Bible-based training courses for youth workers & young people (via Root 66) and Bible Weeks for Christians of all backgrounds who want to develop their skills and learn more

● promoting the use of books, downloads, DVDs and CDs so that Keswick's teaching ministry is brought to a wider audience at home and abroad

● producing TV and radio programmes so that superb Bible talks can be broadcast to you at home

● publishing up-to-date details of Keswick's exciting news and events on our website so that you can access material and purchase Keswick products on-line

● publicizing Bible teaching events in the UK and overseas so that Christians of all ages are encouraged to attend 'Keswick' meetings closer to home and grow in their faith

● putting the residential accommodation of the Convention Centre at the disposal of churches, youth groups, Christian organisations and many others, at very reasonable rates, for holidays and outdoor activities in a stunning location

If you'd like more details please look at our website (www.keswickministries.org) or contact the Keswick Ministries office by post, email or telephone as given below.

**Keswick Ministries, Convention Centre, Skiddaw Street,
Keswick, Cumbria, CA12 4BY
Tel: 017687 80075; Fax: 017687 75276;
email: info@keswickministries.org**

Keswick 2012

Week 1: 14th – 20th July
Week 2: 21st – 27th July
Week 3: 28th July – 3rd August

The annual Keswick Convention takes place in the heart of the English Lake District, an area of outstanding natural beauty. It offers an unparalleled opportunity to listen to gifted Bible exposition, meet Christians from all over the world and enjoy the grandeur of God's creation. Each of the three weeks has a series of morning Bible readings, and then a varied programme of seminars, lectures, book cafés, prayer meetings, concerts, drama and other events throughout the day, with evening meetings that combine worship and teaching. There is also a full programme for children and young people, with Week 1 seeing a return of Abide, meetings aimed specifically at those aged 19–24. Prospects will again be running a series of meetings for those with learning difficulties in Week 2. K2, the interactive track for those in their twenties and thirties, also takes place in Week 2. There will be a special track for the Deaf in Week 3, along with the return of Keswick Unconventional, an opportunity to explore more creative and imaginative aspects of Christian spirituality.

The theme for Keswick 2012 is *Going the Distance*
The Bible readings will be given by:
Simon Manchester (Week 1) on John 14–17
Steve Brady (Week 2) on Ephesians
Jeremy McQuoid (Week 3) on 1 Thessalonians

Other confirmed speakers are Christopher Ash, Ian Coffey, Calisto Odede, Dominic Smart, Chris Sinkinson and Mike Raiter.★

★ Speakers' list correct at time of going to press. Check out the website for further details.

Discipleship

Peter Maiden

Every Christian is called to be a disciple, but do we realise this? And what does it mean?

Peter Maiden, after a lifetime of discipleship, shows from his own struggles and experiences that the life of discipleship is a life of relationship – a love between us and Jesus. We are called to servanthood, to being wise in the use of time and money. Then there are things we can do to help ourselves: the spiritual disciplines of prayer, Bible study, fasting; and things we can do to help each other as church communities. Finally, he looks at what it is all for – mission – and who it is all for – Jesus.

978-1-85078-762-4

Godliness from Head to Toe

James

Jonathan Lamb

One of the biggest questions facing Christians today is, 'How do I live wisely?' Given all that we say about the Christian faith, how are we living? Is there an authentic, credible demonstration of Christian faith that works? All these questions – and more – are covered in this study guide, based on the Bible readings given by Jonathan Lamb at the 2009 Keswick Convention. This book takes us to the heart of James's letter: his passion to serve his Lord, Jesus Christ.

978-1-85078-881-2

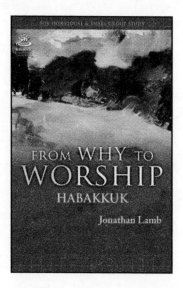

From Why to Worship

Habakkuk

Jonathan Lamb

Jonathan Lamb examines Habbakuk, asking the dem-anding question of whether we can rejoice in the Lord whatever our circumstances.

- Would God be enough if we were to lose everything else?
- Would we be able to say, with Habakkuk, that although we had no means of support, no food, nothing to drink, we would 'rejoice in the Lord'?

This is a challenging book. Jonathan brings Habbakuk's prophecy to life, showing how we can take God with us into our darkest times. Habakkuk wrestles with God: he shouts his questions, roars his unhappiness – and then he waits and lis-tens.

Let Habakkuk take you through your daily life, with all its pains and problems, and find for yourself that the Lord is enough.

978-1-85078-747-1

Authentic

We trust you enjoyed reading this book from Authentic Media Limited. If you want to be informed of any new titles from this author and other exciting releases you can sign up to the Authentic Book Club online:

www.authenticmedia.co.uk/bookclub

Contact us
By Post: Authentic Media Limited
52 Presley Way
Crownhill
Milton Keynes
MK8 0ES

E-mail: info@authenticmedia.co.uk

Follow us: